15 MINUTE
GERMAN
LEARN IN JUST 12 WEEKS

SYLVIA GOULDING

Penguin Random House

Senior Editors Angeles Gavira, Christine Stroyan
Project Art Editor Vanessa Marr
DTP Designer John Goldsmid
Jacket Design Development Manager Sophia MTT
Jacket Designer Juhi Sheth
Pre-Producer David Almond
Senior Producer Ana Vallarino
Associate Publisher Liz Wheeler
Publishing Director Jonathan Metcalf

Language content for Dorling Kindersley by g-and-w publishing.

Produced for Dorling Kindersley by Schermuly Design Co.

First published in Great Britain in 2005.
This revised edition published in 2018 by
Dorling Kindersley Limited
80 Strand, London WC2R 0RL.

A CIP catalogue record is available for this book
from the British Library.
ISBN 978-0-2413-2736-4

Printed in China

A WORLD OF IDEAS:
SEE ALL THERE IS TO KNOW

www.dk.com

CONTENTS

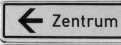

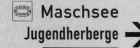

How to use this book

This main part of the book is devoted to 12 themed chapters, broken down into five 15-minute daily lessons, the last of which is a revision lesson. So, in just 12 weeks you will have completed the course. A concluding reference section contains a menu guide and English-to-German and German-to-English dictionaries.

Warm up
Each day starts with a warm up that encourages you to recall vocabulary or phrases you have learned previously. The time in brackets indicates the amount of time you are expected to spend on each exercise.

Instructions
Each exercise is numbered and introduced by instructions that explain what to do. In some cases additional information is given about the language point being covered.

Cultural/Conversational tip
These panels provide additional insights into life in Germany and language usage.

18   WEEK 2

1 Warm up (1 minute)

Count to ten.
(pp.10-11)

Say "hello" and
"goodbye". (pp.8-9)

Ask "Do you have a
brother?" (pp.12-13)

IM CAFÉ
In the café

In a German **Café** the busiest time i when people stop for coffee and cak savoury dishes are also usually availa emphasis is on pastries and gâteaux.

der Zucker
dair tsook-ker
sugar

2 Match and repeat (5 minutes)

Familiarize yourself with the words below. Then test yourself by hiding the German with the cover flap. Practise the words on the picture also.

der Kaffee ohne Milch   black coffee
dair kuf-fay oh-ne milkh

der Tee mit Milch   tea with milk
dair tay mit milkh

das Gebäck   pastry
duss ge-beck

das Sandwich   sandwich
duss zent-vitch

Cultural tip Coffee is always served with milk and sugar, but tea drinkers should specify if they wa milk (**mit Milch**) or lemon (**mit Zitrone**).

3 In conversation (4 minutes)

Ich hätte gern eine
Tasse Tee mit Milch.
ikh het-te gairn ie-ne
tuss-se tay mit milkh

Sonst noch etwas?
zonsst nokh et-vuss

Anything else?

Haber
hah-be

Do you

How to use the flap
The book's cover flaps allow you to conceal the German so that you can test whether you have remembered correctly.

Revision pages
A recap of selected elements of previous lessons helps to reinforce your knowledge.

86   WEEK 8

Antworten
Answers (Cover with flap)

WIEDERHOLUNG
Review and repeat

1 At the office
❶ das Heftgerät
duss heft-ge-rayt
❷ die Lampe
der lam-pe
❸ der Laptop
dair lap-top
❹ der Stift
dair shtift
❺ der Schreibtisch
dair shreip-tish
❻ der Notizblock
dair no-teets-blok
❼ die Uhr
der oor

1 At the office (4 minutes)
Name these items.

3 Work (4 minutes)
Answer these questions followi the numbered English prompts.

Bei welcher Firma
arbeiten Sie?
❶ I work for myself.
Von welcher Universität
sind Sie?
❷ I'm at the University of Köln.
Was ist Ihr Gebiet?
❸ I'm doing medical research.
Haben wir uns auf einen
Zeitplan geeinigt?
❹ Yes, my secretary has
the schedule.

2 Jobs
❶ Arzt/Ärztin
artst/airts-tin
❷ Klempner(in)
klemp-ner(in)
❸ Verkäufer(in)
fer-koy-fer(in)
❹ Buchhalter(in)
bookh-hal-ter(in)
❺ Lehrer(in)
lay-rer(in)
❻ Rechtsanwalt/
Rechtsanwältin
rekhts-an-valt/
rekhts-an-val-tin

2 Jobs (3 minutes)
What are these jobs in German?
❶ doctor
❷ plumber
❸ shop assistant
❹ accountant
❺ teacher
❻ lawyer

4 How much? (4 minutes)
Answer the question with the amount shown in brackets.
❶ Was kostet der
Kaffee? (€2.50)
❷ Was kostet das
Zimmer? (€47)
❸ Was kostet das Kilo
Tomaten? (€3.25)
❹ Was kostet der
Parkplatz für den
Tag? (€10)

ein Stück Kuchen
ine shtewck
koo-khen
slice of cake

der Kaffee
dair kuf-fay
(white) coffee

Useful phrases (5 minutes)

Practise these phrases and then test yourself using the cover flap.

Ich hätte gern eine Tasse Kaffee, bitte.
ikh het-te gairn ie-ne tuss-se kuf-fay, bit-te

I'd like a cup of coffee, please.

Sonst noch etwas?
zonsst nokh et-vuss

Anything else?

Ja, ein Teilchen, bitte.
yah, ine tile-khen, bit-te

Yes, a Danish pastry, please.

Was macht das?
vuss mukht duss

How much is that?

Useful phrases
Selected phrases relevant to the topic help you speak and understand.

Ja, selbstverständlich.
yah, zelpst-fer-shtend-likh

Yes, certainly.

Danke. Was macht das?
dun-ke. vuss mukht duss

Thank you. How much is that?

Vier Euro, bitte.
feer oy-roe, bit-te

Four euros, please.

Text styles
Distinctive text styles differentiate German and English, and the pronunciation guide.

In conversation
Illustrated dialogues reflecting how vocabulary and phrases are used in everyday situations appear throughout the book.

Say it
In these exercises you are asked to apply what you have learned using different vocabulary.

6   Say it (2 minutes)

Do you go near the train station?

The bus station, please.

When's the next coach to Kiel?

Dictionary
A mini-dictionary provides ready reference from English to German and German to English for 2,500 words.

Menu guide
Use this guide as a reference for food terminology and popular German dishes.

Pronunciation guide

Many German sounds will already be familiar to you, but a few require special attention. Take note of how these letters are pronounced:

ch   pronounced from the back of the throat, as in the Scottish *loch*
j   pronounced *y* as in *yes*
r   rolled, produced from the back of the throat
s   pronounced either *s* as in *see* or *z* as in *zoo*
sch pronounced *sh* as in *ship*
ß   a special character that represents a double *ss*
v   pronounced *f* as in *foot*
w   pronounced *v* as in *van*
z/tz pronounced *ts* as in *pets*

German vowels can be tricky, with the same vowel having a number of different pronunciations. Watch out also for these combinations that may look like familiar English sounds, but are pronounced differently in German:

au   as the English *now*
ee   as the English *lay*
ei   as the English *high*
eu   as the English *boy*
ie   as the English *see*

After each word or phrase you will find a pronunciation transcription. Read this, bearing in mind the tips above, and you will achieve a comprehensible result. But remember that the transcription can only ever be an approximation and that there is no real substitute for listening to and mimicking native speakers.

How to use the audio app

All the numbered exercises in each lesson, apart from the Warm ups at the beginning and the Say it exercises at the end, have recorded audio, available via a free app. The app also includes a function to record yourself and listen to yourself alongside native speakers.

To start using the audio with the book, first download the **DK 15 Minute Language Course** app on your smartphone or tablet from the App Store or Google Play. Open the app and scan the QR code on the back of this book to add it to your Library. As soon as the QR code is recognized, the audio will download.

There are two ways in which you can use the audio. The first is to read through your 15-minute lessons using the book only, and then go back and work with the audio and the book together, repeating the text in the gaps provided and then recording yourself. Or you can combine the book and the audio right from the beginning, pausing the app to read the instructions on the page as you need to. Try to say the words aloud, and practise enunciating properly. Detailed instructions on how to use the app are available from the menu bar in the app.

Remember that repetition is vital to language learning. The more often you listen to a conversation or repeat an oral exercise, the more the language will sink in.

Menu, Help/How to Use, Your Library

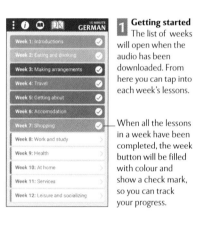

1 Getting started
The list of weeks will open when the audio has been downloaded. From here you can tap into each week's lessons.

When all the lessons in a week have been completed, the week button will be filled with colour and show a check mark, so you can track your progress.

2 Lessons week by week
Each numbered exercise in a lesson is listed in the app as it appears in the book. Tap on an exercise to start.

A check mark indicates when an exercise has been completed.

3 Audio for exercises
Tap the play button to hear instructions, then the exercise. You can pause the audio at any point, and return to it.

You can tap any part of the exercise to play the audio from that point.

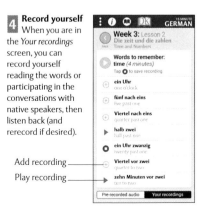

4 Record yourself
When you are in the *Your recordings* screen, you can record yourself reading the words or participating in the conversations with native speakers, then listen back (and rerecord if desired).

Add recording

Play recording

1 Warm up (1 minute)

The Warm Up panel appears at the beginning of each topic. Use it to reinforce what you have already learned and to prepare yourself for moving ahead with the new subject.

GUTEN TAG
Hello

In formal situations, Germans greet each other with a handshake. They are addressed with title **Herr** (*for men*) and **Frau** (*for women*) and last name. Nowadays the title **Fräulein** (*Miss*) is rarely used for adult women. Young people may greet each other with a kiss on each cheek.

2 Words to remember (2 minutes)

Learn these expressions. Conceal the German with the cover flap and test yourself.

Guten Tag. *goo-ten tahk*	Good day/ Hello.
Guten Abend/Nacht. *goo-ten ah-bent/nukht*	Good evening/ night.
Bis bald/morgen. *biss balt/mor-gen*	See you soon/ tomorrow.
Auf Wiedersehen/ Tschüss. *owf vee-der-zay-en/tchews*	Goodbye. (formal/ informal)

Hallo!
hal-loe
Hi!

Cultural tip In addition to proper names, all nouns start with a capital letter in German – for example, **der Tag** (*the day*), as in **Guten Tag** (*good day*).

3 In conversation: formal (3 minutes)

Guten Tag. Ich heiße Martina Li.
goo-ten tahk. ikh high-se mar-teen-a lee

Hello. My name's Martina Li.

Guten Tag. Michael Brand, freut mich.
goo-ten tahk. mikh-ah-ail brant, froyt mikh

Hello. Michael Brand, pleased to meet you.

Freut mich.
froyt mikh

Pleased to meet you.

4 Put into practice (3 minutes)

Join in this conversation. Read the German beside the pictures on the left and then follow the instructions to make your reply. Then test yourself by concealing the answers with the cover flap.

Guten Abend, Herr Gohl.
goo-ten ah-bent, hair goel

Guten Abend.
goo-ten ah-bent

Good evening, Mr Gohl.

Say: Good evening.

Ich heiße Ilse Gerlach.
ikh high-se ilze gair-lakh.

Freut mich.
froyt mikh

My name is Ilse Gerlach.

Say: Pleased to meet you.

5 Useful phrases (3 minutes)

Familiarize yourself with these words. Read them aloud several times and try to memorize them. Conceal the German with the cover flap and test yourself.

What's your name?	**Wie heißen Sie?** *vee high-sen zee*
My name is Thomas.	**Ich heiße Thomas.** *ikh high-se toe-mass*
Pleased to meet you.	**Freut mich.** *froyt mikh*
Thank you.	**Danke.** *dun-ke*

6 In conversation: informal (3 minutes)

Also, bis morgen?
ull-zoe, biss mor-gen

So, see you tomorrow?

Ja, auf Wiedersehen.
yah, owf vee-der-zay-en

Yes, goodbye.

Tschüss. Bis bald.
tchews. biss balt

Goodbye. See you soon.

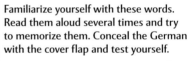

DIE VERWANDTEN
Relatives

1 Warm up (1 minute)

Say "hello" and "goodbye" in German. (pp.8–9)

Now say "My name is...". (pp.8–9)

Say "Mr" and "Mrs". (pp.8–9)

In German things are masculine, feminine, or neuter, taking a different form of "the" according to gender: **der** (*masculine*), **die** (*feminine*), and **das** (*neuter*). There is no easy way of knowing the gender of a word; you will have to memorize them individually.

2 Match and repeat (5 minutes)

Look at the numbered family members in this scene and match them with the vocabulary list at the side. Read the German words aloud. Now, conceal the list with the cover flap and test yourself.

❶ **der Großvater**
  dair groes-fah-ter

❷ **der Bruder**
  dair broo-der

❸ **die Schwester**
  dee shvess-ter

❹ **der Vater**
  dair fah-ter

❺ **die Mutter**
  dee moot-ter

❻ **die Großmutter**
  dee groes-moot-ter

❼ **der Sohn**
  dair zoen

❽ **die Tochter**
  dee tokh-ter

❶ grandfather
brother ❷
❸ sister
❹ father
❺ mother
grandmother ❻
❼ son
❽ daughter

Conversational tip In German the word **ein** (*a/an*) changes according to the gender of the noun - for example, **Ich habe eine Schwester** (*I have a sister*), but **Ich habe einen Sohn** (*I have a son*).

3 Words to remember: relatives (4 minutes)

der Ehemann
dair ay-amunn
husband

die Ehefrau
dee ay-afrow
wife

Ich bin verheiratet.
ikh bin fer-hye-rah-tet
I'm married.

Germans commonly refer to their spouses as **mein Mann** (*my man*) or **meine Frau** (*my woman*). This is not impolite, but a shortened version of **mein Ehemann** and **meine Ehefrau**.

children	**die Kinder** *dee kin-der*
brother-in-law/ sister-in-law	**der Schwager/die Schwägerin** *dair shvar-ger/ dee shvay-ge-rin*
half-brother/ half-sister	**der Halbbruder/ die Halbschwester** *dair hulp-broo-der/ dee hulp-shvess-ter*
stepson/stepdaughter	**der Stiefsohn/die Stieftochter** *dair shteef-zohn/ dee shteef-tokh-ter*
stepfather/stepmother	**der Stiefvater/die Stiefmutter** *dair shteef-fah-ter/ dee shteef-moot-ter*
I have two sons.	**Ich habe zwei Söhne.** *ikh hah-be tsvie zer-ne.*

4 Words to remember: numbers (3 minutes)

Memorize these words and then test yourself using the cover flap.

In German the plural is formed by adding an **en**, **e**, **er**, or **s** to the end of the word, as in **Frau/Frauen** (*woman/women*), **Tag/Tage** (*day/days*), **Mann/Männer** (*man/men*), **Auto/Autos** (*car/cars*). In many cases the main vowel changes to a vowel with an umlaut, as in **der Bruder/die Brüder** (*brother/brothers*). In others there is no change.

one	**eins**	*ients*
two	**zwei**	*tsvie*
three	**drei**	*drie*
four	**vier**	*feer*
five	**fünf**	*fewnf*
six	**sechs**	*zeks*
seven	**sieben**	*zee-ben*
eight	**acht**	*akht*
nine	**neun**	*noyn*
ten	**zehn**	*tsayn*

5 Say it (2 minutes)

One sister.

Three sons.

Two brothers.

1 Warm up (1 minute)

Say the German for as many members of the family as you can. (pp.10-11)

Say "I have two sons". (pp.10-11)

MEINE FAMILIE
My family

There are two ways of saying *you* in German: **Sie** for people you have just met or don't know very well and **du** for family and friends. There are also different words for *your* (see below). It is best to use **Sie** when you first meet someone and wait until he or she invites you to use **du**.

2 Words to remember (5 minutes)

The words for *my* and *your* change, depending on the gender and number of the word to which they relate.

mein *mine*	my (with masculine or neuter)	
meine *mye-ne*	my (with feminine)	
meine *mye-ne*	my (with plural)	
dein *dine*	your (informal, with masculine or neuter)	
deine *dye-ne*	your (informal, with feminine)	
deine *dye-ne*	your (informal, with plural)	
Ihr *eer*	your (formal, with masculine or neuter)	
Ihre *ee-re*	your (formal, with feminine or plural)	

Das sind meine Eltern.
duss zint mye-ne ell-tern
These are my parents.

3 In conversation (4 minutes)

Haben Sie Kinder?
hah-ben zee kin-der

Do you have any children?

Ja, ich habe zwei Töchter.
yah, ikh hah-be tsvie terkh-ter

Yes, I have two daughters.

Hier sind meine Töchter. Und Sie?
heer zint mye-ne terkh-ter. oont zee

These are my daughters. And you?

Conversational tip The most common way to ask a question in German is to invert the verb and the subject: **Sie haben** (*you have*) becomes **Haben Sie...?** (*have you?* or *do you have?*). Similarly, **Sie möchten Kaffee** (*you want coffee*) becomes **Möchten Sie Kaffee?** (*Do you want coffee?*).

4 Useful phrases (3 minutes)

Read these phrases aloud several times and try to memorize them. Conceal the German with the cover flap and test yourself.

Do you have any brothers? (formal)	**Haben Sie Brüder?** *hah-ben zee brew-der*
Do you have any brothers? (informal)	**Hast du Brüder?** *husst doo brew-der*

This is my husband.	**Hier ist mein Mann.** *heer isst mine munn*
That's my wife.	**Dort ist meine Frau.** *dort isst mye-ne frow*

Is that your sister? (formal)	**Ist das Ihre Schwester?** *isst duss ee-re shvess-ter*
Is that your sister? (informal)	**Ist das deine Schwester?** *isst duss dye-ne shvess-ter*

5 Say it (2 minutes)

Do you have any brothers and sisters? (formal)

Do you have any children? (informal)

I don't have any sisters.

This is my wife.

Nein, aber ich habe einen Stiefsohn.
nine, ah-ber ikh hah-be ie-nen shteef-zohn

No, but I have a stepson.

1 Warm up (1 minute)

Say "See you soon".
(pp.8-9)

Say "I am married"
and "I have a wife".
(pp.10-11 and pp.12-13)

SEIN UND HABEN
To be and to have

German verbs have more forms than English ones, so learn them carefully. The verbs **sein** (to be) and **haben** (to have) are used in many expressions, often differently from English. For example, in English you say I'm hungry, but in German you say **Ich habe Hunger** (literally, I have hunger).

2 Sein: to be (5 minutes)

Familiarize yourself with the different forms of **sein** (to be). Use the cover flaps to test yourself and, when you are confident, practise the sample sentences below.

ich bin *ikh bin*	I am
du bist *doo bisst*	you are (informal, singular)
er/sie/es ist *air/zee/ess isst*	he/she/it is
wir sind *veer zint*	we are
ihr seid *eer ziet*	you are (informal, plural)
sie sind/Sie sind *zee zint*	they are/you are (formal)

Ich bin Engländerin.
ikh bin ang-lan-darin
I'm English.

Ich bin müde. *ikh bin mew-de*	I'm tired.
Du bist/Sie sind pünktlich. *doo bisst/zee zint pewnkt-likh*	You're on time.
Ist sie glücklich? *isst zee glewk-likh*	Is she happy?
Wir sind Deutsche. *veer zind doitche*	We're German.

3 Haben (5 minutes)

Haben Sie Brokkoli?
hah-ben zee brokolee
Do you have any broccoli?

Learn this verb and the sample sentences.
Use the flap to test yourself.

I have	**ich habe**	*ikh hah-be*
you have (informal, singular)	**du hast**	*doo husst*
he/she/it has	**er/sie/es hat**	*air/zee/ess hut*
we have	**wir haben**	*veer hah-ben*
you have (informal, plural)	**ihr habt**	*eer hahpt*
they have/you have (formal)	**sie haben/Sie haben**	*zee hah-ben*

He has a meeting.	**Er hat eine Besprechung.**	*air hut ie-ne be-shpre-khoong*
Do you have a mobile phone?	**Haben Sie ein Smartphone?**	*hah-ben zee ine smart-fon*
They have a half-brother.	**Sie haben einen Halbbruder.**	*zee hah-ben ie-nen hulp-broo-der*

4 Negatives (4 minutes)

The most common way to make a sentence negative in German is to put **nicht** (*not*) in front of the word that is negated, much as in English: **Wir sind nicht verheiratet** (*We are not married*). Note the following special negative constructions: *not a/not any* becomes **kein/keine**, *not ever/never* becomes **nie**, and *not anywhere/nowhere* becomes **nirgendwo**.

das Fahrrad
duss fahr-raht
bicycle

Ich habe kein Auto.
ikh hah-be kine ow-to
I don't have a car.

I'm not tired.	**Ich bin nicht müde.**	*ikh bin nikht mew-de*
He's not married.	**Er ist nicht verheiratet.**	*air isst nikht fer-hye-rah-tet*
We don't have any children.	**Wir haben keine Kinder.**	*veer hah-ben kye-ne kin-der*

WIEDERHOLUNG
Review and repeat

Antworten
Answers (Cover with flap)

1 How many?

1 drei
drie

2 neun
noyn

3 vier
feer

4 zwei
tsvie

5 acht
akht

6 zehn
tsayn

7 fünf
fewnf

8 sieben
zee-ben

9 sechs
zeks

1 How many? (2 minutes)

Conceal the answers with the cover flap. Then say these numbers in German. Check you have remembered correctly.

3 ① 9 ② 4 ③
2 ④ 8 ⑤ 10 6 ⑥
5 7 ⑦ 6 ⑨
8 ⑧

2 Hello

1 Guten Tag. Ich heiße...
goo-ten tahk. ikh high-se...

2 Freut mich.
froyt mikh

3 Ja, und ich habe zwei Söhne. Und Sie?
yah, oont ikh hah-be tsvie zer-ne. Oont zee?

4 Auf Wiedersehen. Bis morgen.
owf vee-der-zay-en. biss mor-gen

2 Hello (4 minutes)

You meet someone in a formal situation. Join in the conversation, replying in German according to the English prompts.

Guten Tag. Ich heiße Claudia.
① Answer the greeting and give your name.

Das ist mein Mann, Norbert.
② Say "Pleased to meet you".

Sind Sie verheiratet?
③ Say "Yes, and I have two sons. And you?"

Wir haben drei Töchter.
④ Say "Goodbye. See you tomorrow".

3 To have or be (5 minutes)

Fill in the blanks with the correct form of **haben** (*to have*) or **sein** (*to be*). Check you have remembered the German correctly.

❶ Ich _____ verheiratet.

❷ Sie (*she*) _____ müde.

❸ Wir _____ Deutsche.

❹ _____ Sie eine Besprechung?

❺ Sie (*she*) _____ eine Schwägerin.

❻ Ich _____ kein Handy.

❼ _____ du glücklich?

❽ Das _____ mein Mann.

3 To have or be

❶ **bin**
bin

❷ **ist**
isst

❸ **sind**
zint

❹ **haben**
hah-ben

❺ **hat**
hut

❻ **habe**
hah-be

❼ **bist**
bisst

❽ **ist**
isst

4 Family (4 minutes)

Say the German for each of the numbered family members. Check you have remembered the German correctly.

brother ❷   ❸ sister
grandfather ❶   ❹ father
   ❺ mother

grandmother ❻   ❼ son   ❽ daughter

4 Family

❶ **der Großvater**
dair groes-fah-ter

❷ **der Bruder**
dair broo-der

❸ **die Schwester**
dee shvess-ter

❹ **der Vater**
dair fah-ter

❺ **die Mutter**
dee moot-ter

❻ **die Großmutter**
dee groes-moot-ter

❼ **der Sohn**
dair zohn

❽ **die Tochter**
dee tokh-ter

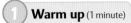

1 Warm up (1 minute)

Count to ten.
(pp.10-11)

Say "hello" and
"goodbye". (pp.8-9)

Ask "Do you have a
brother?" (pp.12-13)

IM CAFÉ
In the café

In a German **Café** the busiest time is the afternoon,
when people stop for coffee and cake. Some
savoury dishes are also usually available, but the
emphasis is on pastries and gâteaux.

der Zucker
dair tsook-ker
sugar

2 Match and repeat (5 minutes)

Familiarize yourself with the words below.
Then test yourself by hiding the German
with the cover flap. Practise the words on
the picture also.

der Kaffee ohne Milch *dair kuf-fay oh-ne milkh*	black coffee
der Tee mit Milch *dair tay mit milkh*	tea with milk
das Gebäck *duss ge-beck*	pastry
das Sandwich *duss zent-vitch*	sandwich

der schwarze Tee
dair shvar-tse tay
black tea

Cultural tip Coffee is always served with milk
and sugar, but tea drinkers should specify if they want
milk (**mit Milch**) or lemon (**mit Zitrone**).

3 In conversation (4 minutes)

**Ich hätte gern eine
Tasse Tee mit Milch.**
*ikh het-te gairn ie-ne
tuss-se tay mit milkh*

I would like a cup of
tea with milk, please.

Sonst noch etwas?
zonsst nokh et-vuss

Anything else?

Haben Sie Kuchen?
hah-ben zee koo-khen

Do you have any cake?

4 Useful phrases (5 minutes)

Practise these phrases and then test yourself using the cover flap.

ein Stück Kuchen
*ine shtewck
koo-khen*
slice of cake

Ich hätte gern eine Tasse Kaffee, bitte.
ikh het-te gairn ie-ne tuss-se kuf-fay, bit-te

I'd like a cup of coffee, please.

Sonst noch etwas?
zonsst nokh et-vuss

Anything else?

Ja, ein Teilchen, bitte.
yah, ine tile-khen, bit-te

Yes, a Danish pastry, please.

Was macht das?
vuss mukht duss

How much is that?

der Kaffee
dair kuf-fay
(white) coffee

Ja, selbstverständlich.
yah, zelpst-fer-shtend-likh

Yes, certainly.

Danke. Was macht das?
dun-ke. vuss mukht duss

Thank you. How much is that?

Vier Euro, bitte.
feer oy-roe, bit-te

Four euros, please.

① Warm up (1 minute)

How do you say "I'd like"? (pp.18-19)

Say "I don't have a brother". (pp.14-15)

Is "der" masculine or feminine? When do you use "die"? (pp.10-11)

IM RESTAURANT
In the restaurant

There are many different eating places in Germany. A **Gaststätte** serves local or international dishes. In a **Gasthof** you'll get a more homely style of cooking. **Ratkeller**, in the basements of historic town halls, serve regional specialities. A **Weinstube** has local wine and snacks.

② Words to remember (3 minutes)

Memorize these words. Conceal the German with the cover flap and then test yourself.

die Speisekarte *dee shpie-ze-kar-te*	menu
die Weinkarte *dee vine-kar-te*	wine list
die Vorspeisen *dee for-shpie-zen*	starters
die Hauptgerichte *dee howpt-ge-rikh-te*	main courses
der Nachtisch *dair nahkh-tish*	desserts
das Mittagessen *duss mit-tahks-ess-sen*	lunch
das Abendessen *duss ah-bent-ess-sen*	dinner
das Frühstück *duss frew-shtewk*	breakfast

cup ❼

saucer ❽

❺ spoon

❻ knife

❹ fork

③ In conversation (4 minutes)

Einen Tisch für vier Personen.
ie-nen tish fewr feer pair-zoe-nen

A table for four.

Haben Sie reserviert?
hah-ben zee re-zair-veert

Do you have a reservation?

Ja, auf den Namen Schmidt.
yah, owf dayn nah-men shmitt

Yes, in the name of Schmidt.

4 Match and repeat (5 minutes)

Look at the numbered items and match them with the German words at the side. Read the German words aloud. Now, conceal the German with the cover flap and test yourself.

① glass

② napkin

① **das Glas**
duss glahss

② **die Serviette**
dee zair-vee-ett-te

③ **der Teller**
dair tell-ler

④ **die Gabel**
dee gah-bell

⑤ **der Löffel**
dair lerff-fel

⑥ **das Messer**
duss mess-ser

⑦ **die Tasse**
dee tuss-se

⑧ **die Untertasse**
dee unter-tuss-se

5 Useful phrases (2 minutes)

Learn these phrases and then test yourself using the cover flap to conceal the German.

plate **③**

What do you have for dessert?	**Was haben Sie zum Nachtisch?** *vuss hah-ben zee tsoom nahkh-tish*
May I have the bill, please.	**Könnte ich bitte die Rechnung haben.** *kern-te ikh bit-te dee rekh-noong hah-ben*

Welchen Tisch möchten Sie?
vel-khen tish merkh-ten zee

Which table would you like?

Am Fenster, bitte.
um fens-ter, bit-te

Near the window, please.

Selbstverständlich. Folgen Sie mir.
zelpst-fer-shtend-likh. fol-gen zee meer

But of course. Follow me.

MÖGEN
To want

1 Warm up (1 minute)

What are "breakfast", "lunch", and "dinner" in German? (pp.20-1)

Say "I", "you" (informal, singular), "he", "she", "it", "we", "you" (formal), "they". (pp.14-15)

In this section, you will learn a verb, **mögen** (to want), which is essential to everyday conversation, as well as a useful polite expression, **ich hätte gern** (I would like). Remember to use this form when requesting something because **ich möchte** (I want) may sound too forceful.

2 Mögen: to want (6 minutes)

Say the different forms of **mögen** (to want) aloud and practise the sample sentences below. Use the cover flaps to test yourself.

ich möchte *ikh merkh-te*	I want
du möchtest *doo merkh-test*	you want (informal, singular)
er/sie/es möchte *air/zee/ess merkh-te*	he/she/it wants
wir möchten *veer merkh-ten*	we want
ihr möchtet *eer merkh-tet*	you want (informal, plural)
sie möchten/Sie möchten *zee merkh-ten*	they want/you want (formal)
Möchtest du Wein? *merkh-test doo vine*	Do you want some wine?
Sie möchte ein neues Auto haben. *zee merkh-te ine noy-es ow-to hah-ben*	She wants a new car.
Wir möchten in Urlaub fahren. *veer merkh-ten in oor-lowp fah-ren*	We want to go on holiday.

Ich möchte Bonbons haben.
ikh merkh-te bom-bongs hah-ben
I want some sweets.

Conversational tip In German you don't need to say *some* as in *We want some ice lollies* for **Wir möchten Eis am Stiel haben**. The phrase *some* is **ein paar**. It is generally used only when you want to imply some but not all, as in **Ich habe nur ein paar Bonbons gegessen**.

3 Polite requests (4 minutes)

It is polite to use the expression **ich hätte gern** (*I would like*) to explain what you would like.

I'd like a beer. **Ich hätte gern ein Bier.**
ikh het-te gairn ine beer

I'd like a table for tonight. **Ich hätte gern einen Tisch für heute abend.**
ikh het-te gairn ie-nen tish fewr hoy-te ah-bent

I'd like the menu. **Ich hätte gern die Speisekarte.**
ikh het-te gairn dee shpie-ze-kar-te

4 Put into practice (4 minutes)

Join in this conversation. Read the German beside the pictures on the left and then follow the instructions to make your reply in German. Test yourself by concealing the answers with the cover flap.

Guten Abend. Haben Sie reserviert?
goo-ten ah-bent. hah-ben zee re-zair-veert

Good evening. Do you have a reservation?

Say: No, but I would like a table for three.

Nein, aber ich hätte gern einen Tisch für drei Personen.
nine, ah-ber ikh het-te gairn ie-nen tish fewr drie per-zoe-nen

Welchen Tisch möchten Sie?
vel-khen tish merkh-ten zee

Which table would you like?

Say: Near the window, please.

Am Fenster, bitte.
um fens-ter, bit-te

DIE GERICHTE
Dishes

1 **Warm up** (1 minute)

Say "I am tired".
(pp.14-15)

Ask "Do you have
pastries?" (pp.18-19)

Say "I'd like a black
coffee". (pp.18-19)

Germany is famous for its sausages and meat dishes
as well as its sauerkraut and dumplings. Today's
restaurants, however, offer a wide selection of
international dishes. Although traditionally the
cuisine is meat-based, many restaurants now
offer vegetarian dishes.

Cultural tip In most restaurants at lunchtime you
will usually have the choice of eating a **Tagesgericht**
(*dish of the day*) or of choosing **à la carte** from the menu.

2 **Match and repeat** (4 minutes)

Look at the numbered items and match them to the
German words in the panel on the left. Test yourself
using the cover flap.

1 das Gemüse
duss ge-mew-ze

2 das Obst
duss opst

3 der Käse
dair kay-ze

4 die Nüsse
dee news-se

5 die Suppe
dee zoop-pe

6 das Geflügel
duss ge-flew-gel

7 der Fisch
dair fish

8 die Nudeln
dee noo-deln

9 die Meeresfrüchte
dee mair-es-frewkh-te

10 das Fleisch
duss fliesh

fruit **2**

vegetables **1**

cheese **3**

5 soup

poultry **6**

8 pasta

9 seafood

3 Words to remember: cooking methods (3 minutes)

Familiarize yourself with these words and then test yourself.

fried	**gebraten**	ge-brah-ten
grilled	**gegrillt**	ge-grillt
roasted	**geröstet**	ge-rerss-tet
boiled	**gekocht**	ge-kokht
steamed	**gedämpft**	ge-dempft
rare	**blutig**	bloo-tikh

Ich hätte mein Steak gern durchgebraten.
ikh het-te mine shtayk gairn doorkh-ge-brah-ten
I'd like my steak well done.

4 Say it (2 minutes)

What is **Sauerbraten**?

I'm allergic to seafood.

I'd like a fruit juice.

nuts ④

5 Words to remember: drinks (3 minutes)

Familiarize yourself with these words.

water	**das Wasser**	duss vuss-ser
fizzy water	**das Wasser mit Kohlensäure**	duss vuss-ser mit koe-len-zoy-re
still water	**das Wasser ohne Kohlensäure**	duss vuss-ser oe-ne koe-len-zoy-re
wine	**der Wein**	dair vine
fruit juice	**der Fruchtsaft**	dair frookht-zufft

fish ⑦

① meat

6 Useful phrases (2 minutes)

Learn these phrases and then test yourself.

I am a vegetarian.	**Ich bin Vegetarier/Vegetarierin.** *ikh bin vay-ge-tah-ree-er/vay-ge-tah-ree-er-in*
I am allergic to nuts.	**Ich bin allergisch gegen Nüsse.** *ikh bin ull-lair-gish gay-gen news-se*
What is "Spätzle"?	**Was ist "Spätzle"?** *vuss isst shpets-le*

WIEDERHOLUNG
Review and repeat

1 What food?

❶ die Nüsse
dee news-se

❷ die Meeresfrüchte
dee mair-es-frewkh-te

❸ das Fleisch
duss fliesh

❹ der Zucker
dair tsook-ker

❺ das Glas
duss glahss

1 What food? (4 minutes)

Name the numbered items.

❶ nuts

❷ seafood

❸ meat

❹ suga

glass ❺

2 This is my...

❶ Das ist mein Ehemann.
duss ist mine ay-emunn

❷ Hier ist meine Tochter.
heer ist mye-ne tokh-ter

❸ Meine Kinder sind müde.
mye-ne kin-der zint mew-de

2 This is my... (4 minutes)

Say these phrases in German.
Use **mein** or **meine**.

❶ This is my husband.

❷ Here is my daughter.

❸ My children are tired.

3 I'd like...

❶ Ich hätte gern Kuchen.
ikh het-te gairn koo-khen

❷ Ich hätte gern einen schwarzen Tee.
ikh het-te gairn ie-nen shvar-tsen tay

❸ Ich hätte gern einen Kaffee.
ikh het-te gairn ie-nen kuf-fay

3 I'd like... (3 minutes)

Say you'd like the following:

cake ❶

❷ black tea

coffee ❸

6 pasta
knife **7**
8 cheese
beer **10**
9 napkin

Answers (Cover with flap)

1 What food?

6 die Nudeln
dee noo-deln

7 das Messer
duss mess-ser

8 der Käse
dair kay-ze

9 die Serviette
dee zair-vee-ett-te

10 das Bier
duss beer

4 Restaurant (4 minutes)

You arrive at a restaurant. Join in the conversation,
replying in German following the English prompts.

Guten Tag.
1 Ask for a table for six.

Raucher oder Nichtraucher?
2 Say: non-smoking.

Folgen Sie mir, bitte.
3 Ask for the menu.

Möchten Sie die Weinkarte?
4 Say: No. Fizzy water, please.

Bitte schön.
5 Say: I don't have a glass.

4 Restaurant

1 Guten Tag. Ich hätte
gern einen Tisch für
sechs Personen.
*goo-ten tahk. ikh het-
te gairn ie-nen tish
fewr zeks pair-zoe-nen*

2 Nichtraucher.
nikht-row-kher

3 Die Speisekarte,
bitte.
*dee shpie-ze-kar-te,
bit-te*

4 Nein. Wasser mit
Kohlensäure, bitte.
*nine. vuss-ser mit koe-
len-zoy-re, bit-te*

5 Ich habe kein Glas.
ikh hah-be kine glahss

DIE TAGE UND DIE MONATE
Days and months

Days of the week and months are all masculine. **Die Woche** (*week*) is feminine. You use **im** with months: **im April** (*in April*), and **am** with days: **am Montag** (*on Monday*). You also use **am** with **Wochenende** (*weekend*).

---

2 **Words to remember: days of the week** (5 minutes)

Familiarize yourself with these words and test yourself using the flap.

Montag *moen-tahk*	Monday
Dienstag *deens-tahk*	Tuesday
Mittwoch *mit-vokh*	Wednesday
Donnerstag *don-ners-tahk*	Thursday
Freitag *frie-tahk*	Friday
Samstag *zumss-tahk*	Saturday
Sonntag *zonn-tahk*	Sunday
heute *hoy-te*	today
morgen *mor-gen*	tomorrow
gestern *guess-tern*	yesterday

Morgen ist Montag.
mor-gen isst moen-tahk
Tomorrow is Monday.

---

3 **Useful phrases: days** (2 minutes)

Learn these phrases and then test yourself using the cover flap.

Die Besprechung ist am Dienstag. *dee be-shpre-khoong isst am deens-tahk*	The meeting is on Tuesday.
Ich arbeite sonntags. *ikh ar-bie-te zonn-tahks*	I work on Sundays.

4 Words to remember: months (5 minutes)

Familiarize yourself with these words and test yourself using the flap.

Ostern ist im April.
oess-tairn isst im ah-prill
Easter is in April.

**Weihnachten ist
im Dezember.**
*vie-nahkh-ten isst im
day-tsem-bair*
Christmas is in December.

January	**Januar** *yunn-oo-ahr*
February	**Februar** *fay-broo-ahr*
March	**März** *mairts*
April	**April** *ah-prill*
May	**Mai** *mie*
June	**Juni** *yoo-nee*
July	**Juli** *yoo-lee*
August	**August** *ow-goosst*
September	**September** *zep-tem-bair*
October	**Oktober** *ok-toe-bair*
November	**November** *noe-vem-bair*
December	**Dezember** *day-tsem-bair*
month	**der Monat** *dair moenat*
day	**der Tag** *dair tahk*

5 Useful phrases: months (2 minutes)

Learn these phrases and then test yourself using the cover flap.

My children are on holiday in August.

**Meine Kinder haben
im August Ferien.**
*mye-ne kin-der hah-ben
im ow-goosst fay-ree-en*

My birthday is in June.

**Mein Geburtstag ist
im Juni.**
*mine ge-boorts-tahk isst
im yoo-nee*

DIE ZEIT UND DIE ZAHLEN
Time and numbers

1 Warm up (1 minute)

Count in German from 1 to 10. (pp.10-11)

Say "I have a reservation". (pp.20-1)

Say "The meeting is on Wednesday". (pp.28-9)

Germans use the 12-hour clock in everyday conversation and the 24-hour clock in official contexts such as timetables. Note that in German half past five is expressed as **halb sechs** (literally, *half six*).

2 Words to remember: time (4 minutes)

Familiarize yourself with these words.

ein Uhr *ine oor*	one o'clock
fünf nach eins *fewnf nahkh ients*	five past one
Viertel nach eins *feer-tel nahkh ients*	quarter past one
halbs zwei *hulp tsvie*	half past one
ein Uhr zwanzig *ine oor tsvun-tsik*	twenty past one
Viertel vor zwei *feer-tel for tsvie*	quarter to two
zehn Minuten vor zwei *tsayn mee-noo-ten for tsvie*	ten to two

3 Useful phrases (2 minutes)

Learn these phrases and then test yourself using the cover flap.

Wie spät ist es? *vee shpayt isst es*	What time is it?

Wann möchten Sie frühstücken? *vunn merkh-ten zee frew-shtewk-ken*	What time do you want breakfast?

Die Besprechung ist um 12 Uhr. *dee be-shpre-khoong isst oom tsverlf oor*	The meeting is at midday.

4 Words to remember: higher numbers (6 minutes)

In German, units are said before tens, so 32 is **zweiunddreißig** (literally, *two-plus-thirty*). Because of this, Germans often write numbers starting at the right and working towards the left.

Ich habe viele Bücher.
ikh hah-be fee-le bew-kher
I have many books.

Das macht fünfundachtzig Euro.
duss makht fewnf-oont-akh-tsik oy-roe
That's eighty-five euros.

eleven	**elf**	*elf*
twelve	**zwölf**	*tsverlf*
thirteen	**dreizehn**	*drie-tsayn*
fourteen	**vierzehn**	*feer-tsayn*
fifteen	**fünfzehn**	*fewnf-tsayn*
sixteen	**sechzehn**	*zekh-tsayn*
seventeen	**siebzehn**	*zeep-tsayn*
eighteen	**achtzehn**	*akh-tsayn*
nineteen	**neunzehn**	*noyn-tsayn*
twenty	**zwanzig**	*tsvun-tsik*
thirty	**dreißig**	*drie-ssik*
forty	**vierzig**	*feer-tsik*
fifty	**fünfzig**	*fewnf-tsik*
sixty	**sechzig**	*zekh-tsik*
seventy	**siebzig**	*zeep-tsik*
eighty	**achtzig**	*akh-tsik*
ninety	**neunzig**	*noyn-tsik*
hundred	**hundert**	*hoon-dairt*
three hundred	**dreihundert**	*drie-hoon-dairt*
thousand	**tausend**	*tow-zent*
ten thousand	**zehntausend**	*tsayn-tow-zent*
two hundred thousand	**zweihunderttausend**	*tsvie-hoon-dairt-tow-zent*
one million	**eine Million**	*ie-ne mill-ee-oen*

5 Say it (2 minutes)

twenty-five

sixty-eight

eighty-four

ninety-one

It's five to ten.

It's half past eleven.

What time is lunch?

DIE TERMINE
Appointments

Business in Germany is generally conducted
more formally than in the UK or the US. Business
associates generally call each other by their title
and last name and use the formal form of *you*,
Sie. Appointments are usually fixed using the
24-hour clock, **fünfzehn Uhr** (*3 pm*).

Willkommen.
vil-komm-men
Welcome.

2 Useful phrases (5 minutes)

Learn these phrases and then test yourself.

Können wir uns morgen treffen? *kernen veer oons mor-gen treff-fen*	Can we meet tomorrow?
Mit wem? *mit vaym*	With whom?
Wann sind Sie frei? *vunn zint zee frie*	When are you free?
Es tut mir Leid, ich bin beschäftigt. *es toot meer liet, ikh bin be-sheff-tikht*	I'm sorry, I am busy.
Wie wär's mit Donnerstag? *vee vairs mit don-ners-tahk*	How about Thursday?
Das passt mir gut. *duss pusst meer goot*	That's good for me.

der Händedruck
dair hen-de-drook
handshake

3 In conversation (4 minutes)

Guten Tage. Ich habe einen Termin.
goo-ten tahk. ikh hah-be ie-nen terr-meen

Hello. I have an appointment.

Mit wem, bitte?
mit vaym, bit-te

With whom, please?

Mit Dieter Frenger.
mit dee-ter fren-ger

With Dieter Frenger.

4 Put into practice (5 minutes)

Join in this conversation. Cover up the text on the right and say the answering part of the dialogue in German. Check your answers and repeat if necessary.

Können wir uns am Donnertsag treffen?
kernen veer oons am don-ners-tahk treff-fen
Shall we meet Thursday?

Say: Sorry, I'm busy.

Es tut mir Leid, ich bin beschäftigt.
es toot meer liet, ikh bin be-sheff-tikht

Wann sind Sie frei?
vunn zint zee frie
When are you free?

Say: Tuesday afternoon.

Dienstag Nachmittag.
deens-tahk nahkh-mit-tahk

Das passt mir gut.
duss pusst meer goot
That's good for me.

Ask: At what time?

Um wieviel Uhr?
oom vee-feel oor

Um sechzehn Uhr, wenn es Ihnen passt.
oom zekh-tsayn oor, venn ess ee-nen pusst
At 16.00 hours, if that's good for you.

Say: It's good for me.

Das passt mir gut.
duss pusst meer goot

Sehr gut. Um wieviel Uhr?
zair goot. oom vee-feel oor

Very good. What time?

Um fünfzehn Uhr, aber ich bin etwas verspätet.
oom fewnf-tsayn oor, ah-ber ikh bin et-vuss fer-shpay-tet

At 15.00 hours, but I'm a little late.

Kein Problem. Setzen Sie sich, bitte.
kine pro-blaym. zet-sen zee zikh, bit-te

Don't worry. Sit down, please.

AM TELEFON
On the telephone

1 Warm up (1 minute)

Say "I'm sorry". (pp.32-3)

What is the German for "I'd like an appointment"? (pp.32-3)

Ask "with whom?" in German. (pp.32-3)

Emergency phone numbers are: **Polizei** (police) 110, **Feuerwehr** (fire service), and **Rettungsdienst** (ambulance) 112. Directory enquiries is 118 33 for inland numbers, 118 34 for abroad, and 118 37 for an English-speaking service.

❷ telephone

2 Match and repeat (4 minutes)

Match the numbered items to the German.

❶ **das Ladegerät**
duss lah-de-ge-rayt

❷ **das Telefon**
duss tay-lay-foen

❸ **der Anrufbeantworter**
dair un-roof-bay-unt-vor-ter

❹ **die Kopfhörer**
dee kopf-her-er

❺ **das Smartphone**
duss smart-fon

❻ **die SIM-Karte**
dee seem-kar-te

❶ charger

headphones ❹

❺ mobile

3 In conversation (4 minutes)

Hallo. Elke Rubin am Apparat.
hul-lo. el-ke roo-been umm up-pa-raht

Hello. Elke Rubin speaking.

Guten Tag. Ich möchte bitte Peter Harnisch sprechen.
goo-ten tahk. ikh merkh-te bit-te peeter har-neesh shpre-khen

Hello. I'd like to speak to Peter Harnisch.

Mit wem spreche ich?
mit vaym shpre-khe ikh

Who's speaking?

SIM card **6**

Ich möchte eine SIM-Karte kaufen.
ikh merkh-te ie-ne seem-kar-te kow-fen
I'd like to buy a SIM card.

3 answering machine

4 Useful phrases (4 minutes)

Learn these phrases. Then test yourself using the cover flap.

Ich möchte Monika's Nummer bitte.
ikh merkh-te monikas num-mer bit-te

I'd like the number for Monika.

Ich möchte mit Rita Wolbert sprechen.
ikh merkh-te mit ree-ta vol-bert shpre-khen

I'd like to speak to Rita Wolbert.

Kann ich eine Nachricht hinterlassen?
kunn ikh ie-ne nahkh-rikht hin-ter-luss-sen

Can I leave a message?

Es tut mir Leid, ich habe mich verwählt.
ess toot meer liet, ikh hah-be mikh fer-vaylt

Sorry, I have the wrong number.

5 Say it (2 minutes)

I'd like to speak to Mr Braun.

Hello, Gaby. Meyer speaking.

Mit Norbert Lorenz von der Druckerei Knickmann.
mit nor-bert loe-rents fon dair drook-er-ie knick-munn

Norbert Lorenz of Knickmann Printers.

Es tut mir Leid. Es ist besetzt.
ess toot meer liet. ess isst be-zetst

I'm sorry. The line is busy.

Würden Sie ihn bitten, mich anzurufen?
vewr-den see een bit-ten, mikh un-tsoo-roo-fen

Can he call me back, please?

WIEDERHOLUNG
Review and repeat

1 Sums

❶ sechzehn
zekh-tsayn

❷ neununddreißig
noyn-oont-drie-ssik

❸ dreiundfünfzig
drie-oont-fewnf-tsik

❹ vierundsiebzig
feer-oont-zeep-tsik

❺ neunundneunzig
noyn-oont-noyn-tsik

❻ einundvierzig
ine-oont-feer-tsik

1 Sums (4 minutes)

Say the answers to these sums aloud in German. Then check if you have remembered correctly.

❶ 10 + 6 = ?
❷ 14 + 25 = ?
❸ 66 − 13 = ?
❹ 40 + 34 = ?
❺ 90 + 9 = ?
❻ 46 − 5 = ?

3 Telephones (3 minutes)

What are the numbered items in German?

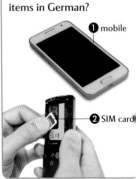

❶ mobile

❷ SIM card

2 I want...

❶ möchten
merkh-ten

❷ möchte
merkh-te

❸ möchten
merkh-ten

❹ möchtest
merkh-test

❺ möchte
merkh-te

❻ möchte
merkh-te

2 I want... (3 minutes)

Fill the gaps with the correct form of **mögen** (to want).

❶ _____ Sie einen Kaffee?

❷ Sie (*singular*) _____ in Urlaub fahren.

❸ Wir _____ einen Tisch für drei Personen.

❹ Du _____ ein Bier.

❺ Ich _____ Bonbons.

❻ Er _____ Obst.

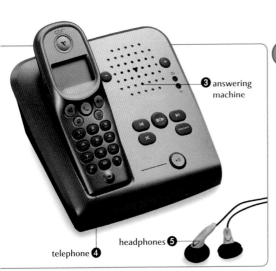

telephone **4**

headphones **5**

answering machine **3**

3 Telephones

1 das Smartphone
das smart-fon

2 die SIM-Karte
dee seem-kar-te

3 der Anrufbeantworter
dair un-roof-bay-unt-vor-ter

4 das Telefon
duss tay-lay-foen

5 die Kopfhörer
dee kopf-her-er

4 When? (2 minutes)

What do these sentences mean?

1 Ich habe einen Termin am Montag, den zwanzigsten Mai.

2 Mein Geburtstag ist im September.

3 Ich arbeite freitags.

4 Sie arbeiten nicht im August.

4 When?

1 I have an appointment on Monday 20th May.

2 My birthday is in September.

3 I work on Fridays.

4 They don't work in August.

5 Time (3 minutes)

Say these times in German.

1 **2** **3**

4 **5** **6**

5 Time

1 ein Uhr
ine oor

2 fünf nach eins
fewnf nahkh ients

3 Viertel nach eins
feer-tel nahkh ients

4 zwanzig Minuten nach eins
tsvun-tsik mee-noo-ten nahkh ients

5 halb zwei
hulp tsvie

6 zehn Minuten vor zwei (Uhr)
tsayn mee-noo-ten for tsvie (oor)

① Warm up (1 minute)

Count to 100 in tens.
(pp.10-11, pp.30-1)

Ask "At what time?"
(pp.32-3)

Say "Half-past one".
(pp.30-1)

AM FAHRKARTENSCHALTER
At the ticket office

On German trains, children under the age of four travel free, and children aged from 4 to 11 years pay half fare. There are also other concessions – for example, for senior citizens, groups, and weekend travel.

② Words to remember (3 minutes)

Learn these words and then test yourself.

der Bahnhof *dair bahn-hoef*	station
der Zug *dair tsook*	train
der Fahrplan *dair fahr-plahn*	timetable
die Fahrkarte *dee fahr-kar-te*	ticket
eine einfache Fahrkarte *ie-ne ine-fa-khe fahr-kar-te*	single ticket
eine Rückfahrkarte *ie-ne rewck-fahr-kar-te*	return ticket
erster/zweiter Klasse *airs-ter/tsvie-ter kluss-se*	first class/ second class

der Bahnsteig
dair bahn-shtiek
platform

das Schild
duss shilt
sign

Der Bahnhof ist überfüllt.
dair bahn-hoef isst ew-ber-fewllt
The station is crowded.

③ In conversation (4 minutes)

Zwei Fahrkarten nach Berlin, bitte.
tsvie fahr-kar-ten nahkh bair-leen, bit-te

Two tickets for Berlin, please.

Rückfahrkarten?
rewck-fahr-kar-ten

Return?

Ja. Muss ich die Sitze reservieren?
yah. mooss ikh dee zit-se re-zair-vee-ren

Yes. Do I need to reserve seats?

4 Useful phrases (5 minutes)

Der Zug hat zehn Minuten Verspätung.
dair tsook hut tsayn mee-noo-ten fer-shpay-toong
The train is ten minutes late.

der Fahrgast
dair fahr-gust
passenger

Learn these phrases and then test yourself using the cover flap.

How much is a ticket to Cologne?	**Was kostet eine Fahrkarte nach Köln?** *vuss kos-tet ie-ne fahr-kar-te nahkh kerln*
Can I pay by credit card?	**Kann ich mit Kreditkarte zahlen?** *kunn ikh mit kray-deet-kar-te tsah-len*
Do I have to change?	**Muss ich umsteigen?** *mooss ikh oomm-shtie-gen*
Which platform does the train leave from?	**Von welchem Bahnsteig fährt der Zug ab?** *fon vel-khem bahn-shtiek fairt dair tsook up*
Are there concessions?	**Gibt es Ermäßigungen?** *geept ess er-mays-si-goong-en*
What time does the train for Dresden leave?	**Wann fährt der Zug nach Dresden ab?** *vunn fairt dair tsook nahkh dres-den up*

5 Say it (2 minutes)

Which platform does the train for Leipzig leave from?

Three return tickets to Hamburg, please.

Cultural tip Most stations have *automatic ticket machines* (**Fahrkartenautomaten**). If you are in a hurry, you can buy tickets on the train, but you won't be able to get any discounts.

Nein. Vierzig Euro, bitte.
nine. feer-tsik oy-roe, bit-te

No. Forty euros, please.

Nehmen Sie Kreditkarten?
nay-men zee kray-deet-kar-ten

Do you accept credit cards?

Ja. Der Zug fährt auf Bahnsteig zehn ab.
yah. dair tsook fairt owf bahn-shtiek tsayn up

Yes. The train leaves from platform ten.

GEHEN UND NEHMEN
To go and to take

1 **Warm up** (1 minute)

Say "train" in German.
(pp.38-9)

What does "von welchem Bahnsteig fährt der Zug ab?" mean?
(pp.38-9)

Ask "When are you free?" (pp.32-3)

Gehen (to go) and **nehmen** (to take) are essential verbs in German, which form part of many useful expressions. Note that these verbs are not always used in the same way as in English and you need to learn phrases individually.

2 **Gehen: to go** (6 minutes)

Say the different forms of **gehen** (to go) aloud. Use the cover flaps to test yourself and, when you are confident, practise the sample sentences below.

ich gehe *ikh gay-e*	I go
du gehst *doo gayst*	you go (informal, singular)
er/sie/es geht *air/zee/ess gayt*	he/she/it goes
wir gehen *veer gay-en*	we go
ihr geht *eer gayt*	you go (informal, plural)
sie gehen/Sie gehen *zee gay-en*	they go/you go (formal)
Wo gehen Sie hin? *voe gay-en zee hin*	Where are you going?
Ich gehe nach Bonn. *ikh gay-e nahhk bonn*	I'm going to Bonn.
Wie geht es Ihnen? *vee gayt ess ee-nen*	How are you?

Ich gehe zum Brandenburger Tor.
ikh gay-e tsoom brun-den-boor-ger tor
I'm going to the Brandenburg Gate.

Conversational tip German uses the same verb form for both *I go* and *I am going*. There is no equivalent of the English present continuous tense, which uses the *-ing* ending. For example, **Ich gehe nach Hamburg** means both *I am going to Hamburg* and *I go to Hamburg*. The same is true of other verbs: **Ich nehme den Zug** (*I am taking the train/I take the train*).

3 Nehmen: to take (6 minutes)

Say the different forms of **nehmen** (to take) aloud and then practise the sample sentences below. Use the cover flaps to test yourself.

Ich nehme die Straßenbahn jeden Tag.
ikh nay-me dee shtrahs-sen-bahn yay-den tahk
I take the tram every day.

ich nehme *ikh nay-me*	I take
du nimmst *doo nimmst*	you take (informal, singular)
er/sie/es nimmt *air/zee/ess nimmt*	he/she/it takes
wir nehmen *veer nay-men*	we take
ihr nehmt *eer naymt*	you take (informal, plural)
sie nehmen/Sie nehmen *zee nay-men*	they take/you take (formal)

Ich möchte kein Taxi nehmen. *ikh merkh-te kine tuck-see nay-men*	I don't want to take a taxi.
Nehmen Sie die erste Straße links. *nay-men zee dee airs-te shtrahs-se links*	Take the first on the left.
Er nimmt den Rehbraten. *air nimmt dayn ray-brah-ten*	He'll have the roast venison.

4 Put into practice (2 minutes)

Cover the text on the right and complete the dialogue in German.

Wo gehen Sie hin? *voe gay-en zee hin* Where are you going?	**Ich gehe zum Bahnhof.** *ikh gay-e tsoom bahn-hoef*

Say: I'm going to the station.

Möchten Sie die U-Bahn nehmen? *merkh-ten zee dee oo-bahn nay-men* Do you want to take the metro?	**Nein, wir wollen den Bus nehmen.** *nine. veer vol-len dayn booss nay-men*

Say: No, we want to go by bus.

TAXI, BUS, UND BAHN
Public transport

1 **Warm up** (1 minute)

Ask "Where are you going?" (pp.40–1)

Say "I'm going to the station". (pp.40–1)

Say "fruit" and "cheese". (pp.24–5)

The larger towns have *underground trains* (**U-Bahn**). Many also have *overground trams* (**Straßenbahn**) or *express trains* (**S-Bahn**). In most cases you need to buy and validate your ticket before you start the journey.

2 **Words to remember** (4 minutes)

Familiarize yourself with these words.

der Bus *dair booss*	bus
der Überlandbus *dair ew-ber-lunt-boos*	coach
der Busbahnhof *dair booss-bahn-hoef*	bus station
die Bushaltestelle *dee booss-hal-te-shtel-le*	bus stop
der Fahrpreis *dair fahr-priess*	fare
das Taxi *duss tuck-see*	taxi
der Taxistand *dair tuck-see-shtunt*	taxi rank
die U-Bahnstation *dee oo-bahn-shta-tsee-oen*	underground station

Hält der Bus Nummer hundertzwanzig hier?
helt dair booss noom-mer hoon-dairt-tsvun-tsik heer
Does the number 120 bus stop here?

3 **In conversation: taxi** (2 minutes)

Zum Flughafen, bitte.
tsoom flook-hah-fen, bit-te

The airport, please.

Jawohl, kein Problem.
yah-voel. kine pro-blaym

Yes, no problem.

Können Sie mich bitte hier absetzen?
ker-nen zee mikh bit-te heer up-zet-sen

Can you drop me here, please?

4 Useful phrases (4 minutes)

Practise these phrases and then test yourself using the cover flap.

I would like a taxi to the cathedral.	**Ich hätte gern ein Taxi zum Dom.** *ikh het-te gairn ine tuck-see tsoom doem*
When is the next bus?	**Wann fährt der nächste Bus?** *vunn fairt dair nekh-ste booss*
How do you get to the museum?	**Wie komme ich zum Museum?** *vee kom-me ikh tsoom moo-zay-oom*
How long is the journey?	**Wie lange dauert die Fahrt?** *vee lan-ge dow-airt dee fahrt*
Please wait for me.	**Bitte warten Sie auf mich.** *bit-te vahr-ten zee owf mikh*

Cultural tip All taxis in Germany have meters. You can hail a taxi in the street when the lights are switched on, board one at a taxi rank, or phone for a taxi from your hotel or private address. Round up the fare to tip the driver.

6 Say it (2 minutes)

Do you go near the train station?

The bus station, please.

When's the next coach to Kiel?

5 In conversation: bus (2 minutes)

Fahren Sie in der Nähe vom Museum entlang? *fah-ren zee in dair nay-e fom moo-zay-oom ent-lung*

Do you go near the museum?

Ja. Das kostet achtzig Cent. *yah. duss kos-tet akh-tsik tsent*

Yes. That's 80 cents.

Können Sie mir sagen, wann wir da sind? *ker-nen zee meer zah-gen, vunn veer dah zind*

Can you tell me when we arrive?

AUF DER STRAßE
On the road

German **Autobahnen** (*motorways*) are fast, but on many stretches there is now a speed limit of 130 km/h (80 mph). They are marked with the letter "A" on a blue sign, international expressways are "E" (**Europastraße**) on a green sign, and main roads "B" (**Bundesstraße**) on a white sign.

1 Warm up (1 minute)

How do you say "I have..."? (pp.14-15)

Say "my father", "my sister", and "my parents". (pp.10-11 and pp.12-13)

Say "I'm going to Berlin". (pp.40-1)

2 Match and repeat (4 minutes)

Match the numbered items to the list below and then test yourself.

1 **der Kofferraum**
dair kof-fer-rowm

2 **die Windschutz-scheibe**
dee vint-shoots-shie-be

3 **die Motorhaube**
dee mo-tor-how-be

4 **der Reifen**
dair rie-fen

5 **das Rad**
duss raht

6 **die Tür**
dee tewr

7 **die Stoßstange**
dee shtoess-shtange

8 **die Scheinwerfer**
dee shien-vair-fer

1 boot

wheel **5**

door **6**

bumper **7**

tyre **4**

Cultural tip In Germany it is obligatory to carry with you in the car at all times your driving licence, car registration document, and a valid insurance certificate.

3 Road signs (2 minutes)

die Einbahnstraße
dee ine-bahn-shtrah-se

One way

der Kreisverkehr
dair kries-fer-kair

Roundabout

Vorfahrt achten
for-fahrt akh-ten

Give way

4 Useful phrases (4 minutes)

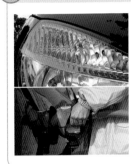

Learn these phrases and then test yourself using the cover flap.

My indicator isn't working.	**Mein Blinker funktioniert nicht.** *mine blin-ker foonk-tsee-oe-neert nikht*
Fill it up, please.	**Volltanken, bitte.** *foll-tan-ken, bit-te*

❷ windscreen

❸ bonnet

headlights ❽

5 Words to remember (3 minutes)

Familiarize yourself with these words and then test yourself using the flap.

petrol	**das Benzin** *duss ben-tseen*
diesel	**der Diesel** *dair dee-zel*
oil	**das Öl** *duss erl*
engine	**der Motor** *dair moe-tor*
gearbox	**das Getriebe** *duss ge-tree-be*
indicator	**der Blinker** *dair blin-ker*
flat tyre	**ein Platten** *ine plutt-ten*
exhaust	**der Auspuff** *dair ows-pooff*
driving licence	**der Führerschein** *dair few-rer-shien*

6 Say it (1 minute)

My gearbox isn't working.

I have a flat tyre.

die Vorfahrtstraße
dee for-fahrt-shtrah-se

Priority route

Einfahrt verboten
ine-fahrt fer-boe-ten

No entry

Parken verboten
par-ken fer-boe-ten

No parking

Antworten
Answers (Cover with flap)

WIEDERHOLUNG
Review and repeat

1 Transport

❶ **der Bus**
dair booss

❷ **das Taxi**
duss tuk-see

❸ **das Auto**
duss ow-toe

❹ **das Fahrrad**
duss fahr-raht

❺ **der Zug**
dair tsook

1 Transport (3 minutes)

Name these forms of transport in German.

bus ❶

❷ taxi

❺ train

2 Go and take

❶ **gehe**
gay-e

❷ **geht**
gayt

❸ **nehme**
nay-me

❹ **gehen**
gay-en

❺ **nehmen**
nay-men

❻ **gehen**
gay-en

2 Go and take (4 minutes)

Use the correct form of the verb in brackets.

❶ Ich ____ zum Bahnhof. (gehen)

❷ Wie ____ es dir? (gehen)

❸ Ich ____ den Rehbraten. (nehmen)

❹ Wir ____ nach Berlin. (gehen)

❺ ____ Sie die erste Straße links. (nehmen)

❻ Wo ____ Sie hin? (gehen)

3 car

4 bicycle

3 Du or Sie?
(4 minutes)

Use the correct form of *you*.

1 You are in a café. Ask "Do you have any cake?"

2 You are with a friend. Ask "Do you want a beer?"

3 A stranger approaches you at your company reception. Ask "Do you have an appointment?"

4 You are on the bus. Ask "Do you go near the station?"

5 Ask your mother where she's going.

3 Du or Sie?

1 Haben Sie Kuchen?
hah-ben zee koo-khen

2 Möchtest du ein Bier?
merkh-test doo ine beer

3 Haben Sie einen Termin?
hah-ben zee ie-nen terr-meen

4 Fahren Sie in der Nähe vom Bahnhof entlang?
fah-ren zee in dair nay-e fom bahn-hoef ent-lung

5 Wo gehst du hin?
voe gayst doo hin

4 Tickets (4 minutes)

You're buying tickets at a train station. Follow the conversation, replying in German with the help of the numbered English prompts.

Kann ich Ihnen helfen?
1 I'd like two tickets to Berlin.

Rückfahrkarte oder einfach?
2 Return, please.

Bitte schön. Fünfzig Euro, bitte.
3 What time does the train leave?

Um dreizehn Uhr zehn.
4 What platform does the train leave from?

Bahnsteig sieben.
5 Thank you very much. Goodbye.

4 Tickets

1 Ich hätte gern zwei Fahrkarten nach Berlin.
ikh het-te gairn tsvie fahr-kar-ten nahkh bair-leen

2 Rückfahrkarte, bitte.
rewck-fahr-kar-te, bit-te

3 Wann fährt der Zug ab?
vunn fairt dair tsook up

4 Von welchem Bahnsteig fährt der Zug ab?
fon vel-khem bahn-shtiek fairt dair tsook up

5 Vielen Dank. Auf Wiedersehen.
fee-len dunk. owf vee-der-zay-en

IN DER STADT
About town

Most German towns still have a market day and a thriving community of small shops. Even small villages tend to have a mayor and a town hall. Parking is usually regulated. Look out for blue parking zones, where you can park your car for a limited time without charge.

1 **Warm up** (1 minute)

Ask "How do you get to the museum?" (pp.42-3)

Say "I want to take the bus" and "I don't want to take a taxi". (pp.40-1)

2 **Match and repeat** (4 minutes)

Match the numbered locations to the words in the panel.

❶ **das Rathaus**
duss raht-hows

❷ **die Brücke**
dee brew-ke

❸ **die Kirche**
dee keer-khe

❹ **der Parkplatz**
dair park-pluts

❺ **das Stadtzentrum**
duss shtutt-tsen-troom

❻ **der Platz**
dair pluts

❼ **die Kunstgalerie**
dee koonst-gal-le-ree

❽ **das Museum**
duss moo-zay-oom

3 **Words to remember** (4 minutes)

Familiarize yourself with these words.

die Tankstelle *dee tunk-shtel-le*	petrol station
das Verkehrsbüro *duss fer-kairs-bew-roe*	tourist information
die Werkstatt *dee vairk-shtutt*	car repairs
das Schwimmbad *duss shvim-bad*	swimming pool
die Bibliothek *dee beeb-lee-o-tayk*	library

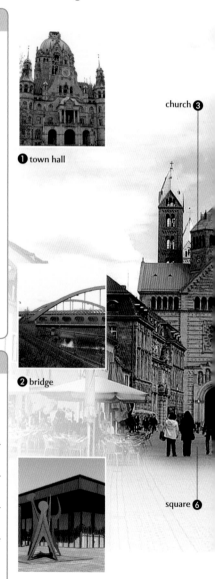

❶ town hall

church ❸

❷ bridge

square ❻

❼ art gallery

4 Useful phrases (4 minutes)

A useful expression for asking about public amenities is **es gibt** (*there is*). Notice that some words are often contracted in German – for example, **in dem** (*in the*) is contracted to **im**; **zu dem** (*to the*, masculine and neuter) becomes **zum**; and **zu der** (*to the*, feminine) contracts to **zur**.

Learn these phrases and then test yourself using the cover flap.

Is there an art gallery in town?	**Gibt es eine Kunstgalerie in der Stadt?** *geept es ie-ne koonst-gal-le-ree in dair shtutt*
Is it far from here?	**Ist das weit von hier?** *isst duss viet fon heer*
There is a swimming pool near the bridge.	**Es gibt ein Schwimmbad bei der Brücke.** *es geept ien shvim-bad bie dair brew-ke*
There isn't a library.	**Es gibt keine Bibliothek.** *es geept kie-ne beeb-lee-o-tayk*

car park **4**

town centre **5**

museum **8**

5 Put into practice (2 minutes)

Join in this conversation. Conceal the text on the right with the cover flap and complete the dialogue in German. Check your answers and repeat if necessary.

Kann ich Ihnen helfen? *kunn ikh ee-nen hel-fen* Can I help you?	**Gibt es in der Stadt eine Bibliothek?** *geept es in dair shtutt ie-ne beeb-lee-o-tayk*
Ask: Is there a library in town?	
Nein, aber es gibt ein Museum. *nine, ah-ber es geept ine moo-zay-oom* No, but there's a museum.	**Wie komme ich zum Museum?** *vee kom-me ikh tsoom moo-zay-oom*
Ask: How do I get to the museum?	
Es ist dort. *es isst dort* It's over there.	**Vielen Dank.** *fee-len dunk*
Say: Thank you very much.	

DIE WEGBESCHREIBUNG
Finding your way

1 Warm up (1 minute)

How do you say "near the station"? (pp.42-3)

Say "Take the first on the left". (pp.40-1)

Ask "Where are you going?" (pp.40-1)

In German you use **gehen** (to go) when talking about going somewhere on foot but **fahren** (to drive) when in a car. So *go left* is **Gehen Sie nach links** if you are on foot, but **Fahren Sie nach links** if you are travelling in a car.

2 Useful phrases (4 minutes)

Learn these phrases and then test yourself.

Gehen Sie nach links/rechts *gay-en zee nahkh links/rekhts*	go left/right
auf der linken Seite/ rechten Seite *owf dair lin-ken zie-te/ rekh-ten zie-te*	on the left side/ right side
geradeaus (weiter) *ge-rah-de-ows (vieter)*	(continue) straight on
Wie komme ich zum Schwimmbad? *vee kom-me ikh tsoom shvim-bad*	How do I get to the swimming pool?
die erste (Straße) links *dee airs-te (shtrah-se) links*	first (street) on the left

die Bibliothek
dee beeb-lee-o-tayk
library

die Fußgängerzone
dee foos-gen-ger-tsoe-ne
pedestrian zone

Gehen Sie am Hauptplatz nach links.
gay-en zee am howpt-pluts nahkh links
Turn left at the main square.

3 In conversation (4 minutes)

Gibt es ein Restaurant in der Stadt?
geept es ine res-to-rung in der shtutt

Is there a restaurant in town?

Ja, am Bahnhof.
yah, um bahn-hoef

Yes, near the station.

Wie komme ich zum Bahnhof?
vee kom-me ikh tsoom bahn-hoef

How do I get to the station?

4 Words to remember (4 minutes)

Ich habe mich verlaufen.
ikh hah-be mikh fer-low-fen
I'm lost.

Familiarize yourself with these words and then test yourself using the flap.

traffic lights	**die Ampel** *dee um-pel*
corner	**die Ecke** *dee ek-ke*
street/road	**die Straße** *dee shtrah-se*
main road	**die Hauptstraße** *dee howpt-shtrah-se*
at the end of the street	**am Ende der Straße** *um en-de dair shtrah-se*
(town) map	**der Stadtplan** *dair shtutt-plahn*
flyover	**die Überführung** *dee ew-ber-few-roong*
opposite	**gegenüber** *gay-gen-ew-ber*

Wir sind hier.
veer zint heer
We are here.

der Brunnen
dair broon-nen
fountain

5 Say it (2 minutes)

Go right at the end
of the street.

It's opposite the
museum.

It's ten minutes
by bus.

**Gehen Sie an der Ampel
nach links.**
*gay-en zee un dair um-
pel nahkh links*

Go left at the traffic lights.

Ist es weit?
isst es viet

Is it far?

**Nein, es ist fünf Minuten
zu Fuß.**
*nine, es isst fewnf
mee-noo-ten tsoo fooss*

No, it's five minutes
on foot.

DIE BESICHTIGUNG
Sightseeing

1 Warm up (1 minute)

Say the days of the week in German. (pp.28-9)

How do you say "at six o'clock"? (pp.30-1)

Ask "What time is it?" (pp.30-1)

Museums tend to stay open all day, but have more restricted opening hours in smaller villages where they are often closed on Sundays. Once a week, usually on Wednesdays or Thursdays, the larger museums will stay open till late, while many are closed on Mondays and on public holidays.

2 Words to remember (4 minutes)

Familiarize yourself with these words and test yourself using the flap.

der Führer *dair few-rer*	guidebook
die Eintrittskarte *dee ine-trits-kar-te*	entrance ticket
die Öffnungszeiten *dee erff-noongs-tsie-ten*	opening times
der Feiertag *dair fie-er-tahk*	public holiday
die Ermäßigung *dee er-mes-see-goong*	reduction/ discount

die Führung
dee few-roong
guided tour

Cultural tip Germany observes a number of religious holidays in addition to Christmas and Easter – for example, Whit Monday and Ascension Day. The May bank holiday is always celebrated on 1st May, whatever day of the week it falls on. There are also additional regional holidays.

3 In conversation (3 minutes)

Sind Sie heute Nachmittag geöffnet?
zint zee hoy-te nahkh-mit-tahk ge-erff-net

Do you open this afternoon?

Ja, aber wir schließen um sechzehn Uhr.
yah, ah-ber veer shliee-sen oom zekh-tsayn oor

Yes, but we close at 4 pm.

Gibt es Zugang für Rollstuhlfahrer?
geept es tsoo-gung fewr roll-shtool-fah-rer

Do you have wheelchair access?

4 Useful phrases (3 minutes)

Öffnungszeiten:
Di. - Fr. 11 - 18 Uhr
Sa. + So. 11 - 16 Uhr
(Montags geschlossen)

Learn these phrases and then test yourself using the cover flap.

What time do you open/close?	**Wann öffnen/ schließen Sie?** *vunn erf-nen/shlee-sen zee*
Where are the toilets?	**Wo sind die Toiletten?** *voe zind dee twah-let-ten*
Is there wheelchair access?	**Gibt es Zugang für Rollstuhlfahrer?** *geept es tsoo-gung fewr roll-shtool-fah-rer*

5 Put into practice (4 minutes)

Cover the text on the right and complete the dialogue in German.

Das Museum ist geschlossen.
duss moo-zay-oom isst ge-shlos-sen
The museum is closed.

Ask: Are you open on Mondays?

Sind Sie am Montag geöffnet?
zint zee um moen-tahk ge-erff-net

Ja, aber wir schließen früh.
yah, ah-ber veer shlee-sen frew

Yes, but we close early.

Ask: At what time?

Um wieviel Uhr?
oom vee-feel oor

Ja, da drüben ist ein Fahrstuhl.
yah, dar drew-ben isst ine fahr-shtool

Yes, there's a lift over there.

Danke, ich hätte gern vier Eintrittskarten.
dun-ke, ikh het-te gairn feer ine-trits-kar-ten

Thank you, I'd like four entrance tickets.

Bitte sehr, und der Führer ist gratis.
bit-te zair, oont dair few-rer isst grah-tis

Here you are, and the guidebook is free.

1 Warm up (1 minute)

Say "You're on time".
(pp.14-15)

What's the German for
"ticket"? (pp.38-9)

Say "I am going to New
York". (pp.40-1)

IM FLUGHAFEN
At the airport

Although the airport environment is largely signposted
in English, it will sometimes be useful to be able to ask
your way around the terminal in German. It's a good
idea to make sure you have a few one-euro coins when
you arrive at the airport; you may need to pay for a
baggage trolley.

2 Words to remember (4 minutes)

Familiarize yourself with these words and
test yourself using the flap.

die Gepäckausgabe *dee ge-peck-ows-gah-be*	baggage reclaim
der Abflug *dair up-flook*	departures
die Ankunft *dee un-koonft*	arrivals
der Zoll *dair tsoll*	customs
die Passkontrolle *dee puss-kon-trol-le*	passport control
das Terminal *duss terr-mee-nahl*	terminal
der Flugsteig *dair flook-shtiek*	gate
die Flugnummer *dee flook-noom-mer*	flight number

**Von welchem Flugsteig geht
der Flug 23?**
*fon vel-khem flook-shtiek gayt dair
flook drie-oont-tsvun-tsik*
What gate does flight 23 leave from?

3 Useful phrases (3 minutes)

Learn these phrases and then test yourself
using the cover flap.

Geht der Flug nach Hannover pünktlich ab? *gayt dair flook nahhk hun-no-fer pewnkt-likh up*	Will the flight for Hanover leave on time?
Ich kann mein Gepäck nicht finden. *ikh kunn mine ge-peck nikht fin-den*	I can't find my baggage.

4 Put into practice (3 minutes)

Join in this conversation. Read the German on the left and follow the instructions to make your reply. Then test yourself by concealing the answers with the cover flap.

Guten Abend. Kann ich Ihnen helfen?
goo-ten ah-bent. kunn ikh ee-nen hel-fen

Hello, can I help you?

Ask: Is the flight to Cologne on time?

Geht der Flug nach Köln pünktlich ab?
gayt dair flook nahkh kerln pewnkt-likh up

Ja.
yah
Yes.

Ask: What gate does it leave from?

Von welchem Flugsteig geht er ab?
fon vel-khem flook-shtiek gayt air up

5 Match and repeat (4 minutes)

Match the numbered items to the German words in the panel.

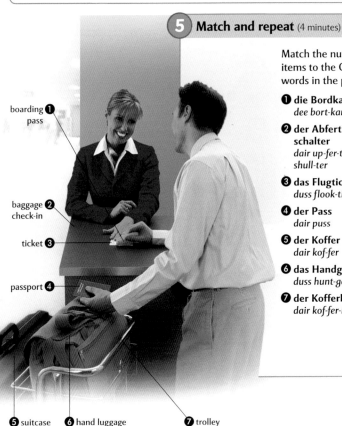

boarding **❶** pass

baggage **❷** check-in

ticket **❸**

passport **❹**

❺ suitcase **❻** hand luggage **❼** trolley

❶ die Bordkarte
dee bort-kar-te

❷ der Abfertigungs-schalter
dair up-fer-ti-goongs-shull-ter

❸ das Flugticket
duss flook-tik-ket

❹ der Pass
dair puss

❺ der Koffer
dair kof-fer

❻ das Handgepäck
duss hunt-ge-peck

❼ der Kofferkuli
dair kof-fer-koo-li

WIEDERHOLUNG
Review and repeat

Antworten
Answers (Cover with flap)

1 Places

❶ **das Museum**
duss moo-zay-oom

❷ **das Rathaus**
duss raht-hows

❸ **die Brücke**
dee brew-ke

❹ **die Kunstgalerie**
dee koonst-gal-le-ree

❺ **der Parkplatz**
dair park-pluts

❻ **der Dom**
dair doem

❼ **der Platz**
dair pluts

1 Places (4 minutes)

Name the numbered places in German.

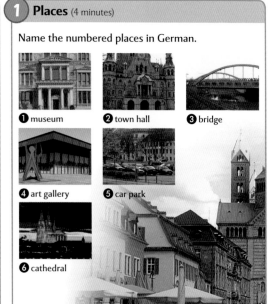

❶ museum   ❷ town hall   ❸ bridge

❹ art gallery   ❺ car park

❻ cathedral

❼ square

2 Car parts

❶ **die Windschutz-scheibe**
dee vint-shoots-shie-be

❷ **der Blinker**
dair blin-ker

❸ **die Motorhaube**
dee mo-tor-how-be

❹ **der Reifen**
dair rie-fen

❺ **die Tür**
dee tewr

❻ **die Stoßstange**
dee shtoess-shtange

2 Car parts (3 minutes)

Name these car parts in German.

windscreen ❶

❺ door
❹ tyre

3 Questions (4 minutes)

Ask the questions in German that match the following answers:

❶ Der Bus fährt um acht Uhr ab.

❷ Kaffee, das macht zwei Euro fünfzig.

❸ Nein, ich möchte keinen Wein.

❹ Der Zug fährt von Bahnsteig fünf ab.

❺ Wir fahren nach Leipzig.

❻ Nein, es ist drei Minuten zu Fuß.

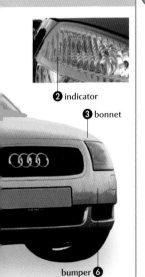

3 Questions

❶ **Wann fährt der Bus ab?**
vunn fairt dair boos up

❷ **Was kostet der Kaffee?**
vuss kos-tet dair kuf-fay

❸ **Möchten Sie Wein?**
merkh-ten zee vine

❹ **Von welchem Bahnsteig fährt der Zug ab?**
fon vel-khem bahn-shtiek fairt dair tsook up

❺ **Wo fahren Sie hin?**
voe fah-ren zee hin

❻ **Ist es weit?**
isst es viet

❷ indicator

❸ bonnet

bumper ❻

4 Verbs (4 minutes)

Choose the correct words to fill the gaps.

❶ Ich ____ Deutsche(r).

❷ Wir ____ mit dem Bus.

❸ Sie *(she)* ____ nach Dresden.

❹ Er ____ drei Töchter.

❺ ____ du Tee?

❻ Wie viele Kinder ____ Sie?

❼ Wo ____ die Toiletten?

4 Verbs

❶ **bin**
bin

❷ **fahren**
fah-ren

❸ **geht**
gayt

❹ **hat**
hut

❺ **möchtest**
merkh-test

❻ **haben**
hah-ben

❼ **sind**
zint

DIE ZIMMER-RESERVIERUNG
Booking a room

1 Warm up (1 minute)

How do you ask in German "Do you accept credit cards?" (pp.38-9)

Ask "How much is that?" (pp.18-19)

How do you ask "Do you have children?" (pp.12-13)

There are different types of accommodation: **das Hotel**, rated by one to five stars; **die Pension** or **der Gasthof**, which are traditional inns; and private accommodation where signs advertise **Zimmer frei** or **Fremdenzimmer**.

2 Useful phrases (3 minutes)

Practise these phrases and then test yourself by concealing the German on the left with the cover flap.

Ist das Frühstück inbegriffen? *isst duss frew-shtewk in-be-grif-fen*	Is breakfast included?

Sind Tiere zugelassen? *zint tee-re tsoo-ge-luss-sen*	Are pets allowed?

Haben Sie Zimmerservice? *hah-ben zee tsim-mer-sair-vis*	Do you have room service?

Wann muss ich das Zimmer freimachen? *vunn mooss ikh duss tsim-mer frie-ma-khen*	When must I vacate the room?

3 In conversation (5 minutes)

Haben Sie noch Zimmer frei?
hah-ben zee nokh tsim-mer frie

Do you have any vacancies?

Ja, ein Doppelzimmer.
yah. ine dop-pel-tsim-mer

Yes, a double room.

Haben Sie ein Kinderbett?
hah-ben zee ine kin-der-bet

Do you have a cot?

4 Words to remember (4 minutes)

Familiarize yourself with these words and test yourself by concealing the German on the right with the cover flap.

Hat das Zimmer Blick auf den Park?
hut duss tsim-mer blick owf dayn park
Does the room have a view over the park?

air-conditioning	**die Klimaanlage**	*dee klee-mah-un-lah-ge*
room	**das Zimmer**	*duss tsim-mer*
single room	**das Einzelzimmer**	*duss ine-tsel-tsim-mer*
double room	**das Doppelzimmer**	*duss dop-pel-tsim-mer*
twin beds	**die zwei Einzelbetten**	*dee tsvie ine-tsel-bet-ten*
bathroom	**das Badezimmer**	*duss bah-de-tsim-mer*
shower	**die Dusche**	*dee doo-she*
breakfast	**das Frühstück**	*duss frew-shtewk*
key	**der Schlüssel**	*dair shlews-sel*
balcony	**der Balkon**	*dair bull-kong*

5 Say it (2 minutes)

Do you have a single room, please?

Does the room have a balcony?

Cultural tip Some, but not all, hotels and guest houses will include breakfast in the price of a room; in others you will be charged extra. Often breakfast is in the style of a **Frühstücksbüffet** (*breakfast buffet*) and includes cereals, a selection of breads, cooked meats, cheeses, jams, fruit juices, and a choice of coffee or tea.

Wie lange möchten Sie bleiben?
vee lun-ge merkh-ten zee blie-ben

How long will you be staying?

Drei Nächte.
drie nekh-te

For three nights.

Sehr gut. Hier ist Ihr Schlüssel.
zair goot. heer isst eer shlews-sel

Very good. Here's your key.

1 Warm up (1 minute)

How do you say "is there...?" and "there isn't..."? (pp.48–9)

What does "Haben Sie reserviert?" mean? (pp.20–1)

IM HOTEL
In the hotel

Although larger hotels almost always have bathrooms en suite, there are still some **Pensionen** and guest houses where you will have to share facilities with other guests. Prices are generally charged for the room, and not per person, so a family staying in one room can be a cheap option.

2 Match and repeat (6 minutes)

Match the numbered items in this hotel bedroom with the German text in the panel and then test yourself using the cover flap.

❶ **der Nachttisch**
dair nukht-tish

❷ **die Lampe**
dee lum-pe

❸ **die Minibar**
dee mini-bar

❹ **die Vorhänge**
dee foer-hen-ge

❺ **die Couch**
dee kowtch

❻ **das Kopfkissen**
duss kopf-kis-sen

❼ **das Kissen**
duss kis-sen

❽ **das Bett**
duss bet

❾ **die Tagesdecke**
dee tah-ges-dek-ke

❿ **die Decke**
dee dek-ke

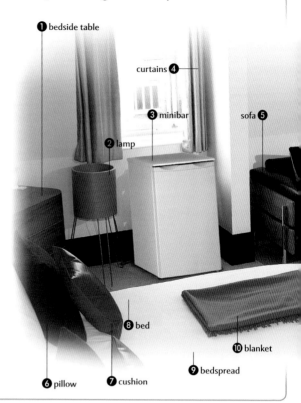

❶ bedside table

curtains ❹

❸ minibar

sofa ❺

❷ lamp

❽ bed

❿ blanket

❾ bedspread

❻ pillow

❼ cushion

Cultural tip Hotel prices vary widely. They are higher during the season in summer or winter resorts. They are often much higher in cities during trade fairs and festivals, such as the Frankfurt Book Fair, the Berlinale Film Festival, the Cologne Carnival, the Hanover Computer Fair CEBIT, and the Munich Beer Festival in October.

3 Useful phrases (5 minutes)

Learn these phrases and then test yourself using the cover flap.

The room is too warm/cold.	**Das Zimmer ist zu warm/kalt.** *duss tsim-mer isst tsoo varm/kullt*

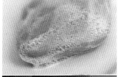

There are no towels.	**Es gibt keine Handtücher.** *es geept kie-ne hunt-tew-kher*

I need some soap.	**Ich brauche Seife.** *ikh brow-khe zie-fe*

The shower doesn't work.	**Die Dusche funktioniert nicht.** *dee doo-she foonk-tsee-oe-neert nikht*

The lift is broken.	**Der Fahrstuhl ist kaputt.** *dair fahr-shtool isst ka-poott*

4 Put into practice (3 minutes)

Cover the text on the right and complete the dialogue in German.

Kann ich Ihnen helfen? **Ich brauche Decken.**
kunn ikh eenen hel-fen *ikh brow-khe dek-ken*

Can I help you?

Say: I need blankets.

Das Zimmermädchen **Und der Fernseher**
wird sie bringen. **ist kaputt.**
duss tsim-mer-met-khen *oont dair fairn-zay-er*
virt zee brin-gen *isst ka-poott*

The maid will bring some.

Say: And the television is broken.

BEIM CAMPING
Camping

1 Warm up (1 minute)

Ask "Can I?" (pp.34-5)

What is English for "the shower"? (pp.60-1)

Say "I need some towels". (pp.60-1)

Camping has long been popular in Germany. There are numerous campsites all over the country, which tend to be of a high standard, usually equipped with washrooms, kitchens, shop, restaurant, and sometimes a swimming pool. Tourist offices have information about sites in their area.

2 Useful phrases (3 minutes)

Learn these phrases. Then test yourself by concealing the German with the cover flap.

Kann ich ein Fahrrad ausleihen? *kunn ikh ine fahr-raht ows-lie-en*	Can I rent a bicycle?
Ist das Wasser trinkbar? *isst duss vuss-ser trink-bahr*	Is this drinking water?
Sind Lagerfeuer erlaubt? *zint lah-ger-foy-er er-lowpt*	Are campfires allowed?
Radios sind verboten. *rah-dee-os zint fer-boe-ten*	Radios are forbidden.

Der Campingplatz ist ruhig.
dair kam-ping-pluts isst roo-hik
The campsite is quiet.

das Campingplatz-büro
duss kamping-plutz-bew-roe
campsite office

das Überzelt
duss ew-ber-tselt
fly sheet

3 In conversation: (5 minutes)

Ich brauche einen Platz für zwei Tage.
ikh brow-khe ie-nen pluts fewr tsvie tah-ge

I need a pitch for two days.

Es gibt einen beim Schwimmbad.
es geept ie-nen bime shvim-bad

There's one near the swimming pool.

Wieviel kostet es für einen Wohnwagen?
vee-feel kos-tet es fewr ie-nen vohn-vah-gen

How much is it for a caravan?

4 Say it (2 minutes)

I need a pitch for four days.

Can I rent a tent?

Where's the electrical hook-up?

der Stromanschluss
dair shtrohm-un-shlooss
electrical hook-up

die Toiletten
dee twah-let-ten
toilets

die Zeltschnur
dee tselt-schnoor
guy rope

der Hering
dair hay-ring
tent peg

5 Words to remember (4 minutes)

Familiarize yourself with these words and test yourself using the flap.

tent	**das Zelt** *duss tselt*
caravan	**der Wohnwagen** *dair voen-vah-gen*
camper van	**das Wohnmobil** *duss voen-moe-beel*
campsite	**der Campingplatz** *dair kam-ping-pluts*
pitch	**der Platz** *dair pluts*
campfire	**das Lagerfeuer** *duss lah-ger-foy-er*
drinking water	**das Trinkwasser** *duss trink-vuss-ser*
rubbish	**der Abfall** *dair up-full*
showers	**die Duschen** *dee doo-shen*
camping gas	**das Campinggas** *duss kam-ping-gahs*
sleeping bag	**der Schlafsack** *dair shlahf-zuck*
air mattress	**die Luftmatratze** *dee looft-mah-trat-se*
ground sheet	**der Zeltboden** *dair tselt-bo-den*

Fünfzig Euro, einen Tag im voraus.
fewnf-tsik oy-roe, ie-nen tahk im for-ows

Fifty euros, one day in advance.

Kann ich einen Grill mieten?
kunn ikh ie-nen grill mee-ten

Can I rent a barbecue?

Ja, aber sie müssen eine Kaution hinterlegen.
yah, ah-ber zee mews-sen ie-ne kow-tsee-oen hin-ter-lay-gen

Yes, but you must pay a deposit.

BESCHREIBUNGEN
Descriptions

Warm up (1 minute)

How do you say "hot" and "cold"? (pp.60-1)

What is the German for "room", "bed", and "pillow"? (pp.60-1)

Simple descriptive sentences are easily constructed in German: **Das Zimmer ist kalt** (*The room is cold*). Note that when adjectives are put first, they may have different endings, such as **-er**, **-e**, **-es**, or **-en** - for example, **ein kaltes Zimmer** (*a cold room*). Just learn these in context as you encounter them.

2 Words to remember (7 minutes)

Learn these words and then test yourself.

hart *hart*	hard
weich *viekh*	soft
heiß *hiess*	hot
kalt *kullt*	cold
groß *groes*	big/tall
klein *kline*	small/short
schön *shern*	beautiful
hässlich *hess-likh*	ugly
laut *lowt*	noisy
ruhig *roo-hig*	quiet
gut *goot*	good
schlecht *shlekht*	bad
langsam *lung-zahm*	slow
schnell *shnell*	fast
dunkel *doon-kel*	dark
hell *hell*	light

Die Berge sind hoch.
dee ber-ge zint hoekh
The mountains are high.

Der Hügel ist niedrig.
dair hew-gel isst nee-drikh
The hill is low.

Die Kirche ist alt.
dee kir-khe isst alt
The church is old.

Das Haus ist klein.
duss hows isst kline
The house is small.

Das Dorf ist sehr schön.
duss dorf isst zair shern
The village is very beautiful.

3 Useful phrases (4 minutes)

To qualify a description add **sehr** (*very*) or **zu** (*too*) in front of the adjective, or surround it with **nicht... genug** (*not... enough*).

This coffee is cold.	**Dieser Kaffee ist kalt.** *dee-zer kuf-fay isst kullt*
My room is very noisy.	**Mein Zimmer ist sehr laut.** *mine tsim-mer isst zair lowt*
My car is too small.	**Mein Auto ist zu klein.** *mine ow-to isst tsoo kline*
The bed is not soft enough.	**Das Bett ist nicht weich genug.** *das bet isst nikht viekh ge-nookh*

4 Put into practice (3 minutes)

Join in this conversation. Cover the text on the right and complete the dialogue in German. Check and repeat if necessary.

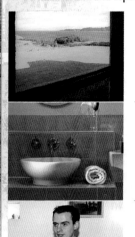

Hier ist das Zimmer. *heer isst duss tsim-mer* Here is the room. Say: The view is very beautiful.	**Die Aussicht ist sehr schön.** *dee ows-zikht isst zair shern*
Dort ist das Badezimmer. *dort isst duss bah-de-tsim-mer* There is the bathroom. Say: It is too small.	**Es ist zu klein.** *es isst tsoo kline*
Wir haben sonst keins. *veer hah-ben zonst keins* We haven't got another. Say: Then we'll take the room.	**Dann nehmen wir das Zimmer.** *dan nay-men veer duss tsim-mer*

WIEDERHOLUNG
Review and repeat

Antworten
Answers (Cover with flap)

1 Adjectives

Adjectives (3 minutes)

What do these sentences mean?

❶ Das Zimmer ist zu heiß.
❷ Mein Kopfkissen ist zu klein.
❸ Der Kaffee ist gut.
❹ Das Badezimmer ist sehr kalt.
❺ Mein Auto ist nicht groß genug.

1 Adjectives

❶ The room is too hot.
❷ My pillow is too small.
❸ The coffee is good.
❹ The bathroom is very cold.
❺ My car is not big enough.

2 Campsite

Campsite (3 minutes)

Name these items you might find in a campsite.

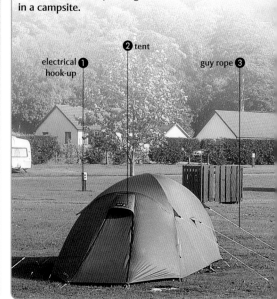

❶ electrical hook-up
❷ tent
❸ guy rope

2 Campsite

❶ der Stromanschluss
dair shtrohm-un-shlooss
❷ das Zelt
duss tselt
❸ die Zeltschnur
dee tselt-shnoor
❹ die Toiletten
dee twah-let-ten
❺ der Wohnwagen
dair voen-vah-gen

3 At the hotel (4 minutes)

You are booking a room in a hotel. Follow the conversation, replying in German following the English prompts.

Kann ich Ihnen helfen?
❶ Do you have any vacancies?

Ja, ein Doppelzimmer.
❷ Are pets allowed?

Ja, wie lange möchten Sie bleiben?
❸ Three nights.

Das macht zweihundertfünfzig Euro.
❹ Is breakfast included?

Selbstverständlich, hier ist der Schlüssel.
　　　　❺ Thank you very much.

3 At the hotel

❶ **Haben Sie noch Zimmer frei?**
hah-ben zee nokh tsim-mer frie

❷ **Sind Tiere zugelassen?**
zint tee-re tsoo-ge-luss-sen

❸ **Drei Nächte.**
drie nekh-te

❹ **Ist das Frühstück inbegriffen?**
isst duss frew-shtewk in-be-grif-fen

❺ **Vielen Dank.**
fee-len dunk

❹ toilets

❺ caravan

4 Negatives (5 minutes)

Make these sentences negative using the verb in brackets.

❶ Ich _____ Kinder. (haben)

❷ Sie _____ morgen nach Hamburg. (fahren)

❸ Er _____ Wein. (möchten)

❹ Ich _____ Zucker in meinem Kaffee. (nehmen)

❺ Die Aussicht _____ sehr schön. (sein)

4 Negatives

❶ **habe keine**
hah-be kie-ne

❷ **fährt nicht**
fairt nikht

❸ **möchte keinen**
merkh-te kie-nen

❹ **nehme keinen**
nay-me kie-nen

❺ **ist nicht**
isst nikht

Warm up (1 minute)

Ask "How do I get to the station?" (pp.50-1)

Say "Turn left at the traffic lights", "Go straight on", "The station is opposite the café". (pp.50-1)

EINKAUFEN
Shopping

Although shopping centres on the outskirts of the cities are increasingly important in Germany, there are still many smaller, traditional, specialized shops. Excellent local markets exist in large cities and small villages. Ask the **Verkehrsbüro** (*tourist office*) when the local market day is held.

Match and repeat (5 minutes)

Match the shops numbered 1-9 on the right to the German in the panel. Then test yourself using the cover flap.

❶ **die Bäckerei**
dee bek-ke-rie

❷ **die Konditorei**
dee kon-dee-to-rie

❸ **das Zeitungskiosk**
duss tsie-toongs-kee-osk

❹ **die Fleischerei**
dee flie-she-rie

❺ **das Feinkostgeschäft**
duss fine-kost-ge-sheft

❻ **die Buchhandlung**
dee bookh-hund-loong

❼ **das Fischgeschäft**
duss fish-ge-sheft

❽ **die Apotheke**
dee a-po-tay-ke

❾ **die Bank**
dee bunk

❶ baker

❷ cake shop

❹ butcher

❺ delicatessen

❼ fishmonger

❽ pharmacy

Cultural tip A German **Apotheke** (*pharmacy*) dispenses both prescription and over-the-counter medicines. It also sells a small range of upmarket health and beauty products. Everyday toiletries such as soap and shampoo are more usually obtained from the **Drogerie**, which is often a self-service supermarket. These shops do not, however, sell medicines of any kind.

3 Words to remember (4 minutes)

Der Blumenladen
dair bloo-men-lah-den
florist

Familiarize yourself with these words and test yourself using the flap.

antique dealer	**der Antiquitätenladen** *dair an-ti-qvi-tay-ten-lah-den*
hairdresser	**der Friseur** *dair fri-zer*
jeweller	**der Juwelier** *dair yoo-ve-leer*
post office	**die Post** *dee posst*
shoe shop	**das Schuhgeschäft** *duss shoo-ge-sheft*
dry cleaner	**die Reinigung** *dee rie-nee-goong*
hardware shop	**der Eisenwarenhändler** *dair ie-zen-vah-ren-hend-ler*

3 newsagent

6 bookshop

9 bank

4 Useful phrases (3 minutes)

Familiarize yourself with these phrases.

Where can I find the hairdresser?	**Wo ist der Friseur?** *voe isst dair fri-zer*
Where do I pay?	**Wo kann ich zahlen?** *voe kunn ikh tsah-len*
Thank you, I'm just looking.	**Danke, ich schaue mich nur um.** *dun-ke, ikh show-e mikh noor oomm*
Do you sell SIM cards?	**Verkaufen Sie SIM-Karten?** *fer-kow-fen zee seem-kar-ten*
I'd like two of these.	**Ich hätte gern zwei von diesen.** *ikh het-te gairn tsvie fon dee-zen*
Is there a department store in town?	**Gibt es in der Stadt ein Kaufhaus?** *geept es in dair shtutt ine kowf-hows*
Can I place an order?	**Kann ich bitte bestellen?** *kunn ikh bit-te be-shtel-len*

5 Say it (2 minutes)

Where can I find the bank?

Do you sell cheese?

I'd like three of these.

AUF DEM MARKT
At the market

1 **Warm up** (1 minute)

What is German for "40", "56", "77", "82", and "94"? (pp.30-1)

Say "I'd like a big room". (pp.64-5)

Ask "Do you have a small car?" (pp.64-5)

Germany uses the metric system of weights and measures. You need to ask for produce in kilogrammes or grammes. You may find that the older generation still use the term **ein Pfund** (*a pound*) meaning half a kilo. Larger items, such as melons, are sold **stückweise** or **am Stück** (*individually*).

2 **Match and repeat** (4 minutes)

Match the numbered items in this scene with the text in the panel.

1 **der Rhabarber**
dair ra-bar-ber

2 **die Kartoffeln**
dee kar-toff-eln

3 **die Radieschen**
dee ra-dees-khen

4 **der Spinat**
dair shpee-naht

5 **die Möhren**
dee mer-ren

6 **der Kohl**
dair koel

7 **der Lauch**
dair lowk

8 **der Kohlrabi**
dair koel-rah-bee

3 radishes

potatoes **2**

rhubarb **1**

cabbage **6**   **8** kohlrabi

7 leeks

3 **In conversation** (3 minutes)

Ich hätte gern Tomaten.
ikh het-te gairn to-mah-ten

I'd like some tomatoes.

Die großen oder die kleinen?
dee groe-sen oe-der dee klie-nen

The large ones or the small ones?

Zwei Kilo kleine, bitte.
tsvie kee-lo klie-ne, bit-te

Two kilos of the small ones, please.

Cultural tip Germany uses the common European currency, the euro, divided into 100 cents. You will usually hear the price as **zehn Euro zwanzig** (€10.20). Often, the word **Euro** is also omitted: **zwei dreißig** (€2.30).

4 Say it (2 minutes)

Three kilos of potatoes, please.

The carrots are too expensive.

How much is the cabbage?

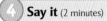

4 spinach

5 carrots

5 Useful phrases (5 minutes)

In German you don't need a word for *of* between the measurement unit (kilo) and the thing you are buying: **ein Kilo Kirschen** (*a kilo of cherries*).

Diese Würstchen sind zu teuer.
dee-ze vewrst-khen zint tsoo toy-er

These sausages are too expensive.

Was kostet ein Kilo Trauben?
vuss kos-tet ine kee-lo-trowben

How much is a kilo of grapes?

Das ist alles.
duss isst ull-les

That's all.

Sonst noch etwas?
zonst nokh et-vuss

Anything else?

Das ist alles, danke. Was kostet das?
duss isst ull-les, dun-ke. vuss kos-tet duss

That's all, thank you. How much?

Drei Euro fünfzig.
drie oy-roe fewnf-tsik

Three euros, fifty.

❶ Warm up (1 minute)

What are these items you could buy in a supermarket? (pp.24–5)

das Fleisch
der Fisch
der Käse
der Fruchtsaft
der Wein
das Wasser

IM SUPERMARKT
At the supermarket

Supermarkets in Germany range from the very well stocked at the expensive end of the market to much cheaper, budget chains. Some larger supermarkets, often in the basement of department stores, have small restaurants where you can sample the produce as you shop.

❷ Match and repeat (5 minutes)

Look at the numbered items and match them to the German words in the panel below. Then test yourself using the cover flap.

❶ **die Haushaltswaren**
dee hows-hults-vah-ren

❷ **das Obst**
duss opst

❸ **die Getränke**
dee ge-tren-ke

❹ **die Fertiggerichte**
dee fair-tikh-ge-rikh-te

❺ **die Kosmetika**
dee kos-may-tee-ka

❻ **die Milchprodukte**
dee milkh-pro-dook-te

❼ **das Gemüse**
duss ge-mew-ze

❽ **die Tiefkühlkost**
dee teef-kewl-kost

household ❶ products
fruit ❷
drinks ❸
ready meals ❹
vegetables ❼
frozen foods ❽

Cultural tip In Germany it is unusual and frowned upon to ask for a plastic bag for your purchases, and you will have to pay for them. Instead, people use their own baskets or re-usable cotton bags that are sold at supermarkets.

3 Useful phrases (3 minutes)

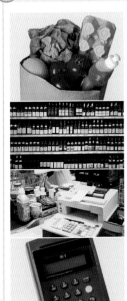

Learn these phrases and then test yourself using the cover flap.

May I have a bag?	**Ich hätte gern eine Tragetasche.** *ikh het-te gairn ie-ne trah-ge-tush-e*
Where is the drinks aisle?	**Wo ist der Gang mit den Getränken?** *voe isst dair gung mit den ge-tren-ken*
Where is the check-out, please?	**Wo ist die Kasse, bitte?** *voe isst dee kuss-se, bit-te*
Please key in your PIN number.	**Bitte geben Sie Ihre Geheimzahl ein** *bit-te gay-ben zee ee-re ge-hime-tsahl ine*

⑤ beauty products

⑥ dairy products

4 Words to remember (4 minutes)

Familiarize yourself with these words and then test yourself.

bread	**das Brot** *duss broet*
milk	**die Milch** *dee milkh*
butter	**die Butter** *dee boott-ter*
ham	**der Schinken** *dair shin-ken*
salt	**das Salz** *duss zullts*
pepper	**der Pfeffer** *dair pfeff-fer*
washing powder	**das Waschpulver** *duss vush-pool-fer*
toilet paper	**das Toilettenpapier** *duss twah-let-ten-pa-peer*
washing-up liquid	**das Geschirrspülmittel** *duss ge-sheerr-shpewl-mit-tel*

5 Say it (2 minutes)

Where's the dairy products aisle?

May I have some ham, please?

Where are the frozen foods?

1 Warm up (1 minute)

Say "I'd like...".
(pp.22-3)

Ask "Do you have...?"
(pp.12-13)

Say "38", "42", and
"46". (pp.30-1)

Say "big" and "small".
(pp.64-5)

BEKLEIDUNG UND SCHUHE
Clothes and shoes

When buying clothes, it is useful to know the colours. In German, colours can be adjectives or nouns; in the latter case they start with a capital: **Der Rock ist rot** (*The skirt is red*) but **Ich nehme diese in Rot** (*I'll take this in red*).

2 Match and repeat (4 minutes)

Match the numbered items of clothing to the German words in the panel below.

1 **das Hemd**
duss hemt

2 **die Krawatte**
dee kra-vutt-te

3 **die Jacke**
dee yuk-ke

4 **die Tasche**
dee ta-she

5 **der Ärmel**
dair airr-mel

6 **die Hose**
dee hoe-ze

7 **der Rock**
dair rok

8 **die Strumpfhose**
dee shtroompf-hoe-ze

9 **die Schuhe**
dee shoo-e

shirt **1**

tie **2**

jacket **3**

pocket **4**

sleeve **5**

trousers **6**

Cultural tip Like most of Europe, Germany uses the continental system of sizes. Dress sizes usually range from 36 (UK 8, US 10) through to 46 (UK 20, US 18) and shoe sizes from 37 (UK 4½, US 6) to 45 (UK 11, US 12). For men's shirts, a size 41 is a 16-inch collar, 43 is a 17-inch collar, and 45 is an 18-inch collar.

3 Useful phrases (3 minutes)

Learn these phrases and then test yourself using the cover flap.

I'll take this in pink.	**Ich nehme das in Rosa.** *ikh nay-me duss in ro-sa*
Do you have this a size larger/ smaller?	**Haben Sie das eine Nummer größer/kleiner?** *hah-ben zee duss ie-ne noom-mer grer-ser/klie-ner*
It's not what I'm looking for.	**Es ist nicht das, was ich suche.** *es isst nikht duss, vuss ikh zoo-khe*

4 Words to remember (5 minutes)

Familiarize yourself with these words and test yourself using the cover flap.

red	**rot** *roet*
white	**weiß** *vies*
blue	**blau** *blow*
yellow	**gelb** *gelp*
green	**grün** *grewn*
black	**schwarz** *shvarts*

7 skirt

8 tights

9 shoes

5 Say it (2 minutes)

Do you have this jacket in black?

Do you have this in a 38?

Do you have a size smaller?

Antworten
Answers (Cover with flap)

WIEDERHOLUNG
Review and repeat

Market

❶ **die Kartoffeln**
dee kar-toff-eln

❷ **die Radieschen**
dee ra-dees-khen

❸ **der Spinat**
dair shpee-naht

❹ **der Kohl**
dair koel

❺ **der Lauch**
dair lowkh

❻ **die Möhren**
dee mer-ren

Market (3 minutes)

Name the numbered items. Conceal the answers with the cover flap and then check if you have remembered the German correctly.

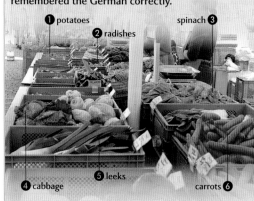

❶ potatoes
❷ radishes
spinach ❸
❹ cabbage
❺ leeks
carrots ❻

Description

❶ These shoes are too expensive.
❷ My room is very small.
❸ The bed is too hard.

Description (2 minutes)

What do these sentences mean?

❶ **Diese Schuhe sind zu teuer.**
❷ **Mein Zimmer ist sehr klein.**
❸ **Das Bett ist zu hart.**

Shops

❶ **die Bäckerei**
dee bek-ke-rie

❷ **die Bank**
dee bunk

❸ **die Buchhandlung**
dee bookh-hund-loong

❹ **das Fischgeschäft**
duss fish-ge-sheft

❺ **die Konditorei**
dee kon-dee-to-rie

❻ **die Fleischerei**
dee flie-she-rie

Shops (3 minutes)

Name the numbered shops in German. Then check your answers.

❶ baker
❷ bank
❸ bookshop

❹ fishmonger
❺ cake shop
❻ butcher

4 **Supermarket** (3 minutes)

Name the numbered items.
Cover the answers with the flap
and then check if you have
remembered correctly.

1 household products

2 beauty products

3 drinks

4 dairy products

5 vegetables

4 **Supermarket**

1 **die Haushalts-
waren**
*dee hows-hults-
vah-ren*

2 **die Kosmetika**
dee kos-may-tee-ka

3 **die Getränke**
dee ge-tren-ke

4 **die Milchprodukte**
*dee milkh-pro-
dook-te*

5 **das Gemüse**
duss ge-mew-ze

5 **Museum** (4 minutes)

Follow this conversation, replying in German with
the help of the numbered English prompts.

Guten Tag. Kann ich Ihnen helfen?
1 I'd like five tickets.

Das macht siebzig Euro.
2 That's very expensive!

Wir geben keine Ermäßigung für Kinder.
3 How much is a guide?

Fünfzehn Euro.
4 Five tickets and a guide, please.

Fünfundachtzig Euro, bitte.
5 Here you are. Where are the toilets?

Dort drüben.
6 Thank you very much.

5 **Museum**

1 **Ich hätte gern
fünf Eintrittskarten.**
*ikh het-te gairn fewnf
ine-trits-kar-ten*

2 **Das ist sehr teuer!**
duss isst zair toy-er

3 **Was kostet
der Führer?**
*vuss kos-tet dair
few-rer*

4 **Fünf Eintrittskarten
und einen Führer,
bitte.**
*fewnf ine-trits-kar-
ten oont ie-nen
few-rer, bit-te*

5 **Bitte sehr. Wo
sind die Toiletten?**
*bit-te zair. voe zint
dee twah-let-ten*

6 **Vielen Dank.**
fee-len dunk

BERUFE
Jobs

Ask "Which platform?"
(pp.38–9)

What is the German for
the following family
members: sister, brother,
mother, father, son, and
daughter? (pp.10–11)

Most job titles are masculine. They can be turned
into the feminine equivalent by adding **-in**: for
example, **der Lehrer/die Lehrerin** (*male/female
teacher*). You don't need to use the indefinite
article *a* when you describe your job: **Ich bin
Buchhalter** (*I'm an accountant*).

2 **Words to remember: jobs** (7 minutes)

The feminine ending is shown in brackets. Some jobs
change the main vowel to an umlaut for the feminine
form: **Arzt/Ärztin** (*male/female doctor*).

Arzt/Ärztin *artst/airts-tin*	doctor
Zahnarzt/Zahnärztin *tsahn-artst/ tsahn-airts-tin*	dentist
Krankenpfleger/ Krankenschwester *krunk-en-pflay-ger/ krunk-en-shves-ter*	nurse
Lehrer(in) *lay-rer(in)*	teacher
Buchhalter(in) *bookh-hull-ter(in)*	accountant
Rechtsanwalt/ Rechtsanwältin *rekhts-un-vullt/ rekhts-un-vel-tin*	lawyer
Grafiker(in) *grah-fi-ker(in)*	designer
Berater(in) *be-rah-ter(in)*	consultant
Sekretär(in) *zek-re-tair(in)*	secretary
Verkäufer(in) *fer-koy-fer(in)*	shop assistant
Elektriker(in) *ay-lek-tree-ker(in)*	electrician
Klempner(in) *klemp-ner(in)*	plumber
selbstständig *zelpst-shten-dikh*	self-employed

Ich bin Klempner.
ikh bin klemp-ner
I'm a plumber.

Sie ist Lehrerin.
zee isst lay-re-rin
She's a teacher.

3 Put into practice (4 minutes)

Practise these phrases. Then cover up the text on the right and complete the dialogue in German.

Was machen Sie beruflich?
vuss ma-khen zee be-roof-likh

What do you do?

Say: I am a consultant.

Ich bin Berater.
ikh bin be-rah-ter

Bei welcher Firma arbeiten Sie?
bie vel-kher fir-ma ar-bie-ten zee

What company do you work for?

Say: I'm self-employed.

Ich bin selbstständig.
ikh bin zelpst-shten-dikh

Wie interessant!
vee in-tay-res-sunt

How interesting!

Ask: And what do you do?

Und was machen Sie beruflich?
oont vuss ma-khen zee be-roof-likh

Ich bin Zahnarzt.
ikh bin tsahn-artst

I'm a dentist.

Say: My sister is a dentist too.

Mein Schwester ist auch Zahnärztin.
mie-ne shves-ter isst owkh tsahn-airts-tin

4 Words to remember: workplace (3 minutes)

Die Zentrale ist in Bremen.
dee tsen-trah-le isst in bray-men
Head office is in Bremen.

Familiarize yourself with these words and test yourself.

head office	**die Zentrale** *dee tsen-trah-le*
branch	**die Zweigstelle** *dee tsviek-shtel-le*
department	**die Abteilung** *dee up-tie-loong*
superior	**der/die Vorgesetzte** *dair/dee for-ge-zets-te*
trainee	**der Auszubildende** *dair ows-tsoo-bilden-de*
reception	**der Empfang** *dair emp-fung*

DAS BÜRO
The office

Warm up (1 minute)

Practise different ways of introducing yourself in different situations. Mention your name, your occupation, and any other information you'd like to give. (pp.8-9, pp.14-15, and pp.78-9)

In all countries, each company has its own special terms, but there are many items that are universal and the English word is often used. Note that the German keyboard has a different layout to the standard QWERTY convention, and that mobile phones are often called **das Handy** (though **das Smartphone** is common too).

Words to remember (5 minutes)

Familiarize yourself with these words. Read them aloud several times and try to memorize them. Conceal the German with the cover flap and test yourself.

der Monitor *dair mo-nee-tor*	monitor
der Computer *dair kom-pyoo-ter*	computer
die Maus *dee mows*	mouse
die E-Mail *dee ee-mayle*	e-mail
das Internet *duss in-ter-net*	internet
das Passwort *duss puss-vort*	password
die Voice-Mail *dee voyse-mayle*	voicemail
der WIFI Code *dair wi-fi kod*	Wi-Fi code
der Fotokopierer *dair fo-to-ko-pee-rer*	photocopier
der Terminkalender *dair terr-meen-ka-len-der*	diary
die Visitenkarte *dee vi-see-ten-kar-te*	business card
die Besprechung *dee be-shpre-khoong*	meeting
die Konferenz *dee kon-fay-rents*	conference
die Tagesordnung *dee tah-ges-ort-noong*	agenda

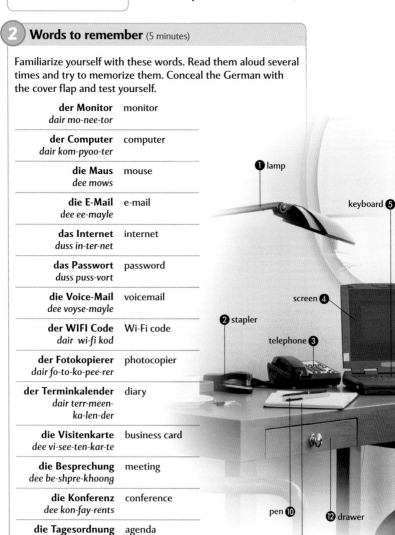

❶ lamp
keyboard ❺
screen ❹
❷ stapler
telephone ❸
pen ❿
⓬ drawer
⓫ notepad

3 Useful phrases (2 minutes)

Learn these phrases and then test yourself using the cover flap.

I need to photocopy something.	**Ich muss etwas fotokopieren.** *ikh mooss et-vuss fo-to-ko-pee-ren*
I'd like to arrange an appointment.	**Ich möchte einen Termin ausmachen.** *ikh merkh-te ie-nen tair-meen ows-ma-khen*
I want to send an e-mail.	**Ich möchte eine E-Mail schicken.** *ikh merkh-te ie-ne ee-mayle shik-ken*

4 Say it (2 minutes)

I'd like to arrange a conference.

I have a laptop.

Do you have a business card?

5 Match and repeat (5 minutes)

Match the numbered items to the words in the panel and test yourself.

6 laptop

7 desk

8 clock

printer 9

13 swivel chair

❶ **die Lampe** *dee lum-pe*

❷ **das Heftgerät** *duss heft-ge-rayt*

❸ **das Telefon** *duss tay-lay-foen*

❹ **der Bildschirm** *dair bilt-sheerm*

❺ **die Tastatur** *dee tuss-tah-toor*

❻ **der Laptop** *dair lap-top*

❼ **der Schreibtisch** *dair shriep-tish*

❽ **die Uhr** *dee oor*

❾ **der Drucker** *dair drook-ker*

❿ **der Stift** *dair shtift*

⓫ **der Notizblock** *dair no-teets-blok*

⓬ **die Schublade** *dee shoop-lah-de*

⓭ **der Drehstuhl** *dair dray-shtool*

DIE AKADEMISCHE WELT
Academic world

1 Warm up (1 minute)

Say "How interesting!" (pp.78-9) and "library". (pp.48-9)

Ask "What do you do?" and answer "I'm an accountant". (pp.78-9)

At German universities, you have to collect credits, often over many years, before you can take the final exam. A first degree is either a **Staatsexamen** (*state exam*) or a **Magister** (*MA*), which can be followed by a **Doktorat** (*PhD*).

2 Useful phrases (3 minutes)

Learn these phrases and then test yourself using the cover flap.

Was ist Ihr Gebiet? *vuss isst eer ge-beet*	What is your field?
Ich betreibe Forschungen in Biochemie. *ikh be-trie-be for-shoong-en in bee-oe-khay-mee*	I am doing research in biochemistry.
Ich habe Jura studiert. *ikh hah-be yoo-ra shtoo-deert*	I studied law.
Ich halte einen Vortrag über moderne Architektur. *ikh hul-te ie-nen vor-trahk ew-ber mo-dair-ne ar-khi-tek-toor*	I am giving a presentation on modern architecture.

3 In conversation (5 minutes)

Guten Tag, ich bin Professor Stein.
goo-ten tahk, ikh bin pro-fes-sor shtien

Hello, I'm Professor Stein.

An welcher Universität arbeiten Sie?
un vel-kher oo-nee-vair-zee-tayt ar-bie-ten zee

What university do you work at?

Ich bin Delegierte der Humboldt-Universität.
ikh bin day-lay-ge-ter dair hoomm-bolt-oo-nee-vair-zee-tayt

I'm the delegate from Humboldt University.

4 Words to remember (4 minutes)

Familiarize yourself with these words and then test yourself.

Wir haben einen Stand.
veer hah-ben ie-nen shtunt
We have a stand.

conference	**die Konferenz** *dee kon-fay-rents*	
trade fair	**die Handelsmesse** *dee hun-dels-mes-se*	
seminar	**das Seminar** *duss zay-mee-nahr*	
lecture theatre	**der Vorlesungssaal** *dair for-lay-zoongs-zahl*	
conference room	**das Konferenzzimmer** *duss kon-fay-rents-tsim-mer*	
exhibition	**die Ausstellung** *dee ows-shtel-loong*	
university lecturer	**der Dozent(in)** *dair do-tsent(in)*	
professor	**der Professor(in)** *dair pro-fes-sor(in)*	
medicine	**die Medizin** *dee may-dee-tseen*	
science	**die Naturwissenschaften** *dee na-toor-vis-sen-shuff-ten*	
humanities	**die Geisteswissen-schaften** *dee gies-tes-vis-sen-shuff-ten*	
engineering	**die Technik** *dee tekh-nik*	

5 Say it (2 minutes)

I'm doing research in medicine.

I studied humanities.

She's the professor.

Was ist Ihr Gebiet?
vuss isst eer ge-beet

What's your field?

Ich betreibe Forschungen in Technik.
ikh be-trie-be for-shoong-en in tekh-nik

I'm doing research in engineering.

Wie interessant!
vee in-tay-res-sunt

How interesting!

GESCHÄFTLICHES
In business

1 Warm up (1 minute)

Ask "Can I...?" (pp.34–5)

Say "I want to send an e-mail". (pp.80-1)

Ask "Can you send a fax?" (pp.80-1)

You will receive a more friendly reception and make a good impression if you make the effort to begin a meeting with a short introduction in German, even if your vocabulary is limited. After that, all parties will probably be happy to continue the meeting in English.

2 Words to remember (6 minutes)

Familiarize yourself with these words and then test yourself by concealing the German with the cover flap.

der Zeitplan *dair tsiet-plahn*	schedule
die Lieferung *dee lee-fe-roong*	delivery
die Bezahlung *dee be-tsah-loong*	payment
das Budget *duss bew-jay*	budget
der Preis *dair priez*	price
die Akte *dee ukk-te*	document
die Rechnung *dee rekh-noong*	invoice
die Zahlen *dee tsah-len*	figures
der Kostenvoranschlag *dair kos-ten-for-un-shlahk*	estimate
der Gewinn *dair ge-vinn*	profits
der Absatz *dair up-zuts*	sales

der Kunde *dair koonn-de* client

Cultural tip Many German companies have **Gleitzeit** (*flexible working hours*). Generally, offices start at 9 am or before, break for lunch at 12 noon, and finish at about 5 pm or earlier. In larger firms and offices, lunch is often taken in a subsidized canteen together with colleagues.

Sollen wir den Vertrag unterzeichnen?
zol-len veer dayn fer-trahk oon-ter-tsiekh-nen
Shall we sign the contract?

die Managerin
dee man-a-je-rin
executive

der Vertrag
dair fer-trahk
contract

3 Useful phrases (6 minutes)

Familiarize yourself with these phrases and then test yourself using the cover flap to conceal the German.

Bitte schicken Sie mir den Vertrag.
bit-te shik-ken zee meer dayn fer-trahk

Please send me the contract.

Haben wir uns auf einen Zeitplan geeinigt?
hah-ben veer oons owf ie-nen tsiet-plahn ge-ie-nikht

Have we agreed a schedule?

Wann können Sie liefern?
vunn kern-nen zee lee-fairn

When can you deliver?

Was ist das Budget?
vuss isst duss bew-jay

What's the budget?

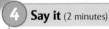
der Bericht
dair be-rikht
report

Können Sie mir die Rechnung schicken?
kern-nen zee meer dee rekh-noong shik-ken

Can you send me the invoice?

4 Say it (2 minutes)

Can you send me the estimate?

Have we agreed on a price?

What are the profits?

Antworten
Answers (Cover with flap)

WIEDERHOLUNG
Review and repeat

1 At the office

❶ **das Heftgerät**
duss heft-ge-rayt

❷ **die Lampe**
dee lum-pe

❸ **der Laptop**
dair lap-top

❹ **der Stift**
dair shtift

❺ **der Schreibtisch**
dair shriep-tish

❻ **der Notizblock**
dair no-teets-blok

❼ **die Uhr**
dee oor

1 At the office (4 minutes)

Name these items.

clock

lamp ❷

❸ laptop

pen ❹

❶ stapler

desk ❺   notepad ❻

2 Jobs

❶ **Arzt/Ärztin**
artst/airts-tin

❷ **Klempner(in)**
klemp-ner(in)

❸ **Verkäufer(in)**
fer-koy-fer(in)

❹ **Buchhalter(in)**
bookh-hull-ter(in)

❺ **Lehrer(in)**
lay-rer(in)

❻ **Rechtsanwalt/**
Rechtsanwältin
rekhts-un-vullt/
rekhts-un-vel-tin

2 Jobs (3 minutes)

What are these jobs in German?

❶ doctor

❷ plumber

❸ shop assistant

❹ accountant

❺ teacher

❻ lawyer

3 Work (4 minutes)

Answer these questions following the numbered English prompts.

Bei welcher Firma arbeiten Sie?
❶ I work for myself.

Von welcher Universität sind Sie?
❷ I'm at the University of Köln.

Was ist Ihr Gebiet?
❸ I'm doing medical research.

Haben wir uns auf einen Zeitplan geeinigt?
❹ Yes, my secretary has the schedule.

3 Work

❶ **Ich bin selbstständig.**
ikh bin zelpst-shten-dikh

❷ **Ich bin von der Universität Köln.**
ikh bin fon dair oo-nee-vair-zee-tayt kewln

❸ **Ich betreibe Forschungen in der Medizin.**
ikh be-trie-be for-shoong-en in dair may-dee-tseen

❹ **Ja, meine Sekretärin hat den Zeitplan.**
yah, mye-ne zek-re-tair-in hut dayn tsiet-plahn

4 How much? (4 minutes)

Answer the question with the amount shown in brackets.

❶ **Was kostet der Kaffee?** (€2.50)

❷ **Was kostet das Zimmer?** (€47)

❸ **Was kostet das Kilo Tomaten?** (€3.25)

❹ **Was kostet der Parkplatz für drei Tage?** (€50)

4 How much?

❶ **Das macht zwei Euro fünfzig.**
duss makht tsvie oy-roe fewnf-tsik

❷ **Es kostet sieben-undvierzig Euro.**
es kos-tet zee-ben-oont-feer-tsik oy-roe

❸ **Das macht drei Euro fünfundzwanzig.**
duss makht drie oy-roe fewnf-oont-tsvun-tsik

❹ **Er kostet fünfzig Euro.**
air kos-tet fewnf-tsik oy-roe

Say "I'm allergic to nuts".
(pp.24–5)

Say the verb **haben**
(to have) in all its forms
(**ich, du er/sie/es, wir,
ihr, sie/Sie**). (pp.14–15)

IN DER APOTHEKE
At the chemist

German *pharmacies* are indicated by a stylized red
letter **A** for **Apotheke**. Pharmacists dispense a wide
variety of medicines over the counter. They advise
and can even give injections, if necessary. In larger
towns, a rota ensures that there is always one
pharmacy that is open.

2 **Match and repeat** (3 minutes)

Match the numbered items to the German
words in the panel below and test yourself
using the cover flap.

❶ der Verband
dair fer-bunt

❷ der Sirup
dair zee-roop

❸ die Tropfen
dee trop-fen

❹ das Pflaster
duss pflus-ter

❺ die Spritze
dee shprit-se

❻ die Salbe
dee zull-be

❼ das Zäpfchen
duss tsepf-khen

❽ die Tablette
dee tub-let-te

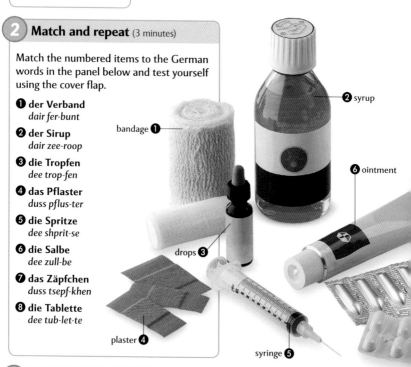

bandage ❶

❷ syrup

❻ ointment

drops ❸

plaster ❹

syringe ❺

3 **In conversation** (3 minutes)

**Guten Tag, Sie
wünschen?**
*goo-ten tahk, zee
vewn-shen*

Hello. What would
you like?

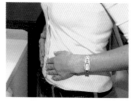

**Ich habe
Bauchschmerzen.**
*ikh hah-be bowkh-
shmairt-sen*

I have a stomach ache.

Haben Sie Durchfall?
hah-ben zee doorkh-full

Do you have
diarrhoea?

4 Words to remember (2 minutes)

In German you don't use the indefinite article *a* to describe a pain.

Ich habe Kopfschmerzen.
ikh hah-be
kopf-shmairt-sen
I have a headache.

headache	**Kopfschmerzen** *kopf-shmairt-sen*
stomach ache	**Bauchschmerzen** *bowkh-shmairt-sen*
diarrhoea	**Durchfall** *doorkh-full*
cold (in the nose)	**der Schnupfen** *dair shnoop-fen*
cough	**der Husten** *dair hoos-ten*
sunburn	**der Sonnenbrand** *dair zon-nen-brunt*
toothache	**Zahnschmerzen** *tsahn-shmairt-sen*

5 Say it (2 minutes)

I have a cold.

Do you have that as an ointment?

Do you have a cough?

7 suppository

8 tablet

6 Useful phrases (4 minutes)

Learn these phrases and then test yourself using the cover flap.

I have sunburn.	**Ich haben einen Sonnenbrand.** *ikh hah-be ie-nen zon-nen-brunt*
Do you have that as a syrup?	**Haben Sie das auch als Sirup?** *hah-ben zee duss owkh ulls zee-roop*
I'm allergic to penicillin.	**Ich bin allergisch gegen Penizillin.** *ikh bin ull-lair-gish gay-gen pay-nee-tsee-leen*

Nein, aber ich habe auch Kopfschmerzen.
nine, ah-ber ikh hah-be owkh kopf-shmairt-sen

No, but I also have a headache.

Nehmen Sie dies.
nay-men zee dees

Take this.

Haben Sie das auch als Tabletten?
hah-ben zee duss owkh ulls tub-let-ten

Do you have that as tablets?

DER KÖRPER
The body

In German many expressions to do with health are reflexive, that is, the equivalent of *I am not feeling well* in German is **Ich fühle mich nicht wohl** (literally, *I am not feeling myself well*). As in English, the reflexive pronoun (*myself, yourself,* etc.) changes, depending on the context.

1 Warm up (1 minute)

Say " I have a toothache" and "I have sunburn". (pp.88-9)

Say the German for "red", "green", "black", and "yellow". (pp.74-5)

2 Match and repeat (6 minutes)

Match the numbered parts of the body with the list below.

❶ **die Hand**
dee hunt

❷ **der Kopf**
dair kopf

❸ **die Schulter**
dee shool-ter

❹ **der Ellbogen**
dair el-bo-gen

❺ **das Haar, die Haare**
duss hahr, dee hah-re

❻ **der Arm**
dair arm

❼ **der Hals**
dair hulls

❽ **die Brust**
dee broost

❾ **der Bauch**
dair bowkh

❿ **das Bein**
duss bine

⓫ **das Knie**
duss k-nee

⓬ **der Fuß**
dair fooss

hand ❶
head ❷
shoulder ❸
❹ elbow
❺ hair
❻ arm
❼ neck
❽ chest
❾ stomach
❿ leg
⓫ knee
⓬ foot

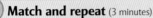

3 Match and repeat (3 minutes)

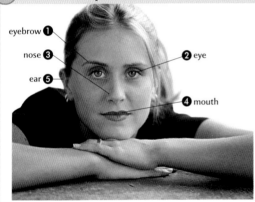

eyebrow ❶

nose ❸

ear ❺

❷ eye

❹ mouth

Match the numbered facial features with the list below.

❶ die Augenbraue
dee ow-gen-brow-e

❷ das Auge
duss ow-ge

❸ die Nase
dee nah-ze

❹ der Mund
dair moont

❺ das Ohr
duss ohr

4 Useful phrases (3 minutes)

Learn these phrases and then test yourself using the cover flap.

I have a pain in my back.	**Ich habe Schmerzen im Rücken.** *ikh hah-be shmairt-sen im rewk-ken*
I have a rash on my arm.	**Ich habe einen Ausschlag am Arm.** *ikh hah-be ie-nen ows-shluk um arm*
I don't feel well.	**Ich fühle mich nicht wohl.** *ikh few-le mikh nikht voel*

5 Put into practice (2 minutes)

Join in this conversation and test yourself using the cover flap.

Was ist denn los?
vuss isst denn loes

What's the matter?

Say: I'm not feeling well.

Ich fühle mich nicht wohl.
ikh few-le mikh nikht voel

Wo tut es denn weh?
voe toot es den vayh

Where does it hurt?

Say: I have a pain in my shoulder.

Ich haben Schmerzen in der Schulter.
ikh hah-be shmairt-sen in dair shool-ter

1 Warm up (1 minute)

Say "I need some tablets" and "He needs some ointment". (pp.60-1 and pp.88-9)

What is the German for "I don't have a son"? (pp.10-15)

BEIM ARZT
At the doctor

German doctors are titled according to their specialist qualifications, such as **Internist** (*internal medicine*) and **Kardiologe** (*heart specialist*). A *general practitioner* is known as **praktischer Arzt**. In most cases you'll need an appointment, or you can visit the hospital outpatients department.

2 Useful phrases you may hear (3 minutes)

Learn these phrases and then test yourself using the cover flap to conceal the German.

Es ist nichts Ernsthaftes. *es isst nikhts airnst-huff-tes*	It's not serious.
Wir müssen ein paar Tests machen. *veer mews-sen ine pahr tests ma-khen*	We need to do a few tests.
Sie haben eine Niereninfektion. *zee hah-ben ie-ne nee-ren-infek-tsee-oen*	You have an infection in your kidney.
Sie müssen ins Krankenhaus gehen. *zee mews-sen ins krunk-en-hows gay-en*	You need to go to hospital.

Nehmen Sie irgend-welche Medikamente?
nay-men zee ir-gent-vel-khe may-dee-ka-men-te
Are you taking any medication?

3 In conversation (5 minutes)

Was ist denn los?
vuss isst den loes

What's the matter?

Ich habe Schmerzen in der Brust.
ikh hah-be shmairt-sen in dair broost

I have a pain in my chest.

Ich werde Sie untersuchen.
ikh vair-de zee oon-ter-zoo-khen

I'll examine you.

4 Useful phrases you may need to say (4 minutes)

Learn these phrases and then test yourself using the cover flap.

I am diabetic.	**Ich bin Diabetiker(in).** *ikh bin dee-ar-bay-ti-kair(in)*
I am epileptic.	**Ich bin Epileptiker(in).** *ikh bin ay-pee-lep-ti-kair(in)*
I have asthma.	**Ich habe Asthma.** *ikh hah-be ast-ma*
I have a heart condition.	**Ich bin herzkrank.** *ikh bin hairts-krunk*
I have a fever.	**Ich habe Fieber.** *ikh hah-be fee-ber*
It's urgent.	**Es ist dringend.** *es isst dring-ent*
I feel faint.	**Ich fühle mich schwach.** *ikh few-le mikh shvakh*
I feel sick.	**Mir ist schlecht.** *meer isst shlekht*

Ich bin schwanger.
ikh bin shvun-ger
I am pregnant.

Cultural tip
If you are an EU national, you can obtain free emergency medical treatment in Germany on production of a valid European Health Insurance Card (EHIC).

5 Say it (2 minutes)

It is serious.

My son needs to go to hospital.

It's not urgent.

Ist es etwas Ernsthaftes?
isst es et-vuss airnst-huff-tes

Is it serious?

Nein, nur Verdauungs-beschwerden.
nine, noor fer-dow-oongs-be-shvair-den

No, only indigestion.

Ein Glück!
ine glewkk

What a relief!

IM KRANKENHAUS
At the hospital

Say "how long" as
in "how long is the
journey?" (pp.42-3)

Ask "Do I need tests?"
(pp.92-3)

Say "mouth" and "head".
(pp.90-1)

It is useful to know a few basic phrases relating to
hospitals for use in an emergency or in case you
need to visit a friend or colleague in hospital.
A *ward* in hospital is known as **die Station**
and the equivalent of the *outpatient
department* is known as **die Ambulanz**.

2 **Useful phrases** (5 minutes)

Familiarize yourself with these phrases.
Conceal the German with the cover flap
and test yourself.

Wann ist Besuchszeit? *vunn isst be-zookhs-tsiet*	What are the visiting hours?
Wie lange wird das dauern? *vee lun-ge virt duss dow-ern*	How long will it take?
Tut das weh? *toot duss vayh*	Will it hurt?
Bitte legen Sie sich hier hin. *bit-te lay-gen zee zikh heer hin*	Please lie down here.
Sie dürfen nichts essen. *zee dewr-fen nikhts es-sen*	You must not eat.
Bewegen Sie nicht den Kopf. *be-vay-gen zee nikht dayn kopf*	Don't move your head.
Bitte öffnen Sie Ihren Mund. *bit-te erf-nen zee ee-ren moont*	Please open your mouth.
Wir müssen eine Blutprobe machen. *veer mews-sen ie-ne bloot-proe-be ma-khen*	We'll have to do a blood test.

Wo ist das Wartezimmer?
voe isst duss var-te-tsim-mer
Where is the waiting room?

die intravenöse Infusion
*dee in-tra-vay-ner-ze
in-foo-zee-oen*
intravenous drip

Geht es Ihnen besser?
gayt es ee-nen bes-ser
Are you feeling better?

3 Words to remember (4 minutes)

Memorize these words and test yourself using the cover flap.

emergency department	**die Unfallstation** *dee oon-full-shtah-tsee-oen*
x-ray department	**die Röntgenabteilung** *dee rernt-gen-up-tie-loong*
children's ward	**die Kinderstation** *dee kin-der-shtah-tsee-oen*
operating theatre	**der Operationssaal (der OP)** *dair o-pay-rah-tsee-oens-zahl (dair oe-pay)*
corridor	**der Gang** *dair gung*
stairs	**die Treppe** *dee trep-pe*

Ihre Rötgenaufhahme ist normal.
ee-re rernt-gen-owf-nah-me isst nor-mal
Your x-ray is normal.

4 Put into practice (3 minutes)

Join in this conversation. Read the German on the left and follow the instructions to make your reply. Then test yourself by concealing the answers with the cover flap.

Sie haben eine Entzündung.
zee hah-ben ie-ne ent-tsewn-doong

You have an infection.

Ask: Will you need to do tests?

Müssen Sie Untersuchungen machen?
mews-sen zee oon-ter-zoo-khoong-en ma-khen

Zuerst machen wir eine Blutprobe.
tsoo-airst ma-khen veer ie-ne bloot-proe-be

First we will do a blood test.

Ask: Will it hurt?

Tut das weh?
toot duss vayh

5 Say it (2 minutes)

Will you need to do a blood test?

Where is the children's ward?

Nein, keine Angst.
nine, kie-ne unkst

No. Don't worry.

Ask: How long will it take?

Wie lange wird das dauern?
vee lun-ge virt duss dow-ern

WIEDERHOLUNG
Review and repeat

1 The body

❶ **der Kopf**
dair kopf

❷ **der Arm**
dair arm

❸ **die Brust**
dee broost

❹ **der Bauch**
dair bowkh

❺ **das Bein**
duss bine

❻ **das Knie**
duss k-nee

❼ **der Fuß**
dair fooss

1 The body (4 minutes)

Name the numbered body parts in German.

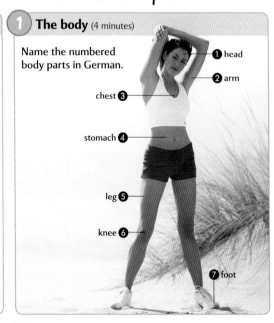

❶ head
❷ arm
chest ❸
stomach ❹
leg ❺
knee ❻
❼ foot

2 On the phone

❶ **Ich möchte bitte Venny Gerlach sprechen.**
ikh merkh-te bit-te ven-nee gair-lakh shpre-khen

❷ **Horst Richter von der Druckerei Gohl.**
horst rikh-ter fon dair drook-er-ie goel

❸ **Kann ich eine Nachricht hinterlassen?**
kunn ikh ie-ne nahkh-rikht hin-ter-luss-sen

❹ **Der Termin für Montag elf Uhr ist in Ordnung.**
dair terr-meen fewr mohn-tahk elf oor isst in ord-noong

2 On the phone (4 minutes)

You are confirming an appointment with a business contact on the telephone. Join in the conversation, replying in German following the English prompts.

Hello, Firma Apex.
❶ I'd like to speak to Venny Gerlach.

Ja, mit wem spreche ich?
❷ Horst Richter of Gohl Printers.

Es tut mir Leid, da ist besetzt.
❸ Can I leave a message?

Aber selbstverständlich.
❹ The appointment on Monday at 11 am is fine.

3 Clothing (3 minutes)

Say the German words for the numbered items of clothing.

tie ❶
❷ jacket
❹ skirt
trousers ❸
❻ tights
shoes ❺

3 Clothing

❶ **die Krawatte**
dee kra-vutt-te

❷ **die Jacke**
dee yuk-ke

❸ **die Hose**
dee hoe-ze

❹ **der Rock**
dair rok

❺ **die Schuhe**
dee shoo-e

❻ **die Strumpfhose**
dee shtroompf-hoe-ze

4 At the doctor's (4 minutes)

Say these phrases in German.

❶ I don't feel well.
❷ Will you need to do tests?
❸ I have a heart condition.
❹ Do I need to go to hospital?
❺ I'm pregnant.

4 At the doctor's

❶ **Ich fühle mich nicht wohl.**
ikh fewh-le mikh nikht voel

❷ **Müssen Sie Untersuchungen machen?**
mews-sen zee oon-ter-zoo-khoong-en ma-khen

❸ **Ich bin herzkrank.**
ikh bin hairts-krunk

❹ **Muss ich ins Krankenhaus gehen?**
mooss ikh ins krunk-en-hows gay-en

❺ **Ich bin schwanger.**
ikh bin shvun-ger

ZU HAUSE
At home

Say the months of
the year in German.
(pp.28-9)

Ask "Is there...?"
(pp.48-9)

Most Germans live in *rented apartments*
(**die Wohnung**); only relatively few own their
homes (**das Eigenheim**). The size of a dwelling is
given in square metres and described in terms of the
number of rooms in addition to kitchen and bathroom:
2 ZKB means **2 Zimmer, Küche, Badezimmer**.

2 **Match and repeat** (5 minutes)

Match the numbered items to the list
below and test yourself using the flap.

❶ **das Dach**
duss dukh

❷ **der Schornstein**
dair shorn-shtine

❸ **die Dachrinne**
dee dukh-rin-ne

❹ **der Blumenkasten**
*dair bloo-men-
kass-ten*

❺ **die Mauer**
dee mow-er

❻ **das Fenster**
duss fens-ter

❼ **die Tür**
dee tewr

❽ **die Straße**
dee shtrah-se

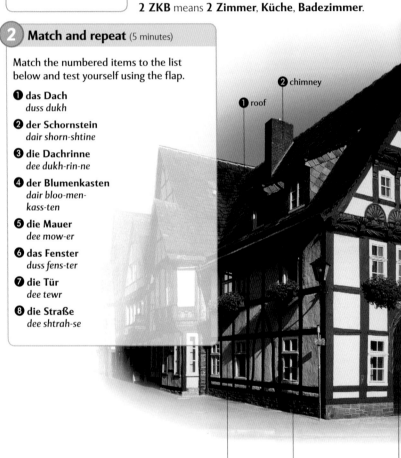

❷ chimney

❶ roof

wall ❺   window ❻   door ❼

Conversational tip In Germany, a detached house is
known as an **Einfamilienhaus** - literally a *one-family house*.
A semi-detached house is called a **Zweifamilienhaus**
(*two-family house*), while a terraced house is called a
Reihenhaus (*house in a row*). The *centre of town* is the
Innenstadt, and a *suburb* is a **Vorstadt** or **Vorort**.

3 Words to remember (4 minutes)

Wie hoch ist die monatliche Miete?
vee hoekh isst dee mo-naht-li-khe mee-te
What is the rent per month?

Familiarize yourself with these words and test yourself using the flap.

room	**das Zimmer** *duss tsim-mer*
floor	**der Fußboden** *dair foos-bo-den*
ceiling	**die Decke** *dee dek-ke*
bedroom	**das Schlafzimmer** *duss shlahf-tsim-mer*
bathroom	**das Badezimmer** *duss bah-de-tsim-mer*
kitchen	**die Küche** *dee kew-khe*
dining room	**das Esszimmer** *duss ess-tsim-mer*
living room	**das Wohnzimmer** *duss vohn-tsim-mer*
cellar	**der Keller** *dair kel-ler*
attic	**der Dachboden** *dair dukh-boe-den*

❸ gutter

❹ window box

❽ roadway

4 Useful phrases (3 minutes)

Learn these phrases and test yourself.

Gibt es eine Garage?
geept es ie-ne ga-ra-je

Is there a garage?

Ab wann ist es frei?
up vunn isst es frie

When is it available?

Ist es möbliert?
isst es mer-bleert

Is it furnished?

5 Say it (2 minutes)

Is there a dining room?

Is it large?

Is it available in July?

IM HAUS
In the house

Warm up (1 minute)

What is the German for "desk" (pp.80–1), "bed" (pp.60–1), and "window"? (pp.98–9)

How do you say "soft", "beautiful", and "big"? (pp.64–5)

If you're renting a flat or a house in Germany, the rent is often described as **kalt** (*cold*). This means that services such as electricity have to be paid for in addition to the basic rent. You will need to check this in advance. *Furnished apartments* in holiday resorts are known as **Ferienwohnung**.

2 Match and repeat (3 minutes)

Match the numbered items to the list in the panel below. Then test yourself by concealing the German with the cover flap.

1 die Arbeitsfläche
dee ar-biets-flay-khe

2 das Spülbecken
duss shpewl-bek-ken

3 die Mikrowelle
dee mee-kro-vel-le

4 der Backhofen
dair bak-oe-fen

5 der Herd
dair hairt

6 der Kühlschrank
dair kewl-shrunk

7 der Stuhl
dair shtool

8 der Tisch
dair tish

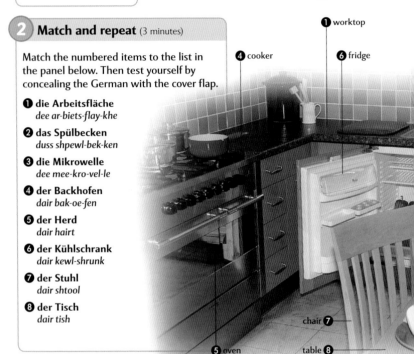

1 worktop
4 cooker
6 fridge
chair **7**
5 oven
table **8**

3 In conversation (3 minutes)

Das ist der Herd.
duss isst dair hairt

This is the cooker.

Gibt es eine Geschirrspülmaschine?
geept es ie-ne ge-sheerr-spewl-mah-shee-ne

Is there a dishwasher?

Ja, und der Gefrierschrank ist groß.
yah, oont dair ge-freer-shrunk isst groes

Yes, and the freezer is big.

4 Words to remember (2 minutes)

Familiarize yourself with these words and test yourself using the flap.

Die Couch ist neu.
dee kowtch isst noy
The sofa is new.

microwave **3**

sink **2**

wardrobe	**der Schrank** *dair shrunk*	
armchair	**der Sessel** *dair zes-sel*	
carpet	**der Teppich** *dair tep-pikh*	
bathtub	**die Badewanne** *dee bah-de-vunn-ne*	
toilet	**die Toilette (das WC)** *dee twah-let-te (duss vay-tsay)*	
wash basin	**das Waschbecken** *duss vush-bek-ken*	
curtains	**die Gardine** *dee gar-dee-ne*	

5 Useful phrases (4 minutes)

Learn these phrases and then test yourself.

The cooker doesn't work.	**Der Herd funktioniert nicht.** *dair hairt foonk-tsee-oe-neert nikht*
I don't like the curtains.	**Die Gardinen gefallen mir nicht.** *dee gar-dee-nen ge-fall-en meer nikht*
Is electricity included?	**Ist der Strom inbegriffen?** *isst dair shtroem in-be-grif-fen*

6 Say it (2 minutes)

Is there a microwave?

I like the carpet.

The bathroom is beautiful!

Ist das Spülbecken neu?
isst duss spewl-bek-ken noy

Is the sink new?

Und hier ist die Waschmaschine.
oont heer isst dee vush-mah-shee-ne

And here's the washing machine.

Die Kacheln sind schön!
dee ka-kheln zint shern

The tiles are beautiful!

DER GARTEN
The garden

Say "I need" and "you need". (pp.92-3)

What is the German for "day" and "month"? (pp.28-9)

Ask "Is there a garage?" (pp.98-9)

Many Germans who live in apartments rent allotment gardens. But rather than just growing fruits and vegetables there, they often turn these into attractive leisure gardens with extensive flowerbeds and ponds as well as terraces, decks, and barbecues for casual entertaining.

2 **Words to remember** (3 minutes)

Familiarize yourself with these words and test yourself using the flap.

der Rasenmäher *dair rah-zen-may-er*	lawnmower
die Gabel *dee gah-bel*	fork
der Spaten *dair shpah-ten*	spade
der Rechen *dair re-khen*	rake
das Gartencenter *duss gar-ten-tsen-ter*	garden centre

2 tree

terrace **1**

plants **6**

8 weeds

path **9**   **3** soil

3 Useful phrases (4 minutes)

Learn these phrases and then test yourself using the cover flap.

The gardener comes once a week.	**Der Gärtner kommt einmal in der Woche.** *dair gairt-ner komt ine-mahl in dair vo-khe*
Can you please mow the lawn?	**Können Sie bitte den Rasen mähen?** *kern-nen zee bit-te dayn rah-zen may-en*
Is the garden private?	**Ist der Garten privat?** *isst dair gar-ten pree-vaht*
The garden needs watering.	**Der Garten muss gegossen werden.** *dair gar-ten mooss ge-gos-sen vair-den*

4 Match and repeat (5 minutes)

Match the numbered items in this garden to the words in the panel.

5 hedge
4 lawn
7 flowers
10 flowerbed

1 die Terrasse
dee ter-ras-se

2 der Baum
dair bowm

3 die Erde
dee air-de

4 der Rasen
dair rah-zen

5 die Hecke
dee hek-ke

6 die Pflanzen
dee pflun-tsen

7 die Blumen
dee bloo-men

8 das Unkraut
duss oon-krowt

9 der Weg
dair vayk

10 das Blumenbeet
duss bloo-men-bayt

5 Say it (2 minutes)

The lawn needs watering.

Are there any trees?

The gardener comes on Fridays.

DIE HAUSTIERE
Pets

1 Warm up (1 minute)

Say "My name's John".
(pp.8-9)

How do you say "Don't
worry"? (pp.94-5)

What's "your" in
German? (pp.12-13)

Pet passports are now available to enable
holiday-makers and commuters to take their
pets with them to Germany and avoid quarantine
on return to the United Kingdom. Consult your
vet for details of how to obtain the necessary
vaccinations and paperwork.

2 Match and repeat (3 minutes)

Match the numbered animals to the
German words below. Test yourself
using the cover flap.

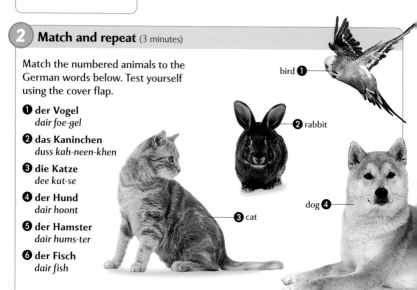

bird ❶

❷ rabbit

dog ❹

❸ cat

❶ **der Vogel**
dair foe-gel

❷ **das Kaninchen**
duss kah-neen-khen

❸ **die Katze**
dee kut-se

❹ **der Hund**
dair hoont

❺ **der Hamster**
dair hums-ter

❻ **der Fisch**
dair fish

3 Useful phrases (4 minutes)

Familiarize yourself with these phrases and
then test yourself using the cover flap.

Ist dieser Hund gutartig? *isst dee-zer hoont goot-ar-tikh*	Is this dog friendly?
Kann ich meinen Hund mitbringen? *kunn ikh mie-nen hoont mit-bring-en*	Can I bring my dog?
Ich habe Angst vor Katzen. *ikh hah-be unkst foer kut-tsen*	I'm frightened of cats.
Mein Hund beißt nicht. *mine hoont biesst nikht*	My dog doesn't bite.

Diese Katze hat Flöhe.
dee-ze kut-se hut fler-we
This cat has fleas.

Cultural tip Many dogs in Germany are working dogs and you may encounter them tethered or roaming free. Approach rural houses with particular care. Look out for warning notices such as **Warnung vor dem Hunde** (*Beware of the dog*).

4 Words to remember (4 minutes)

Meinem Hund geht es nicht gut.
mie-nem hoont gayt es nikht goot
My dog is not well.

5 hamster

fish **6**

Familiarize yourself with these words and test yourself using the flap.

basket	**der Korb** *dair korp*	
cage	**der Käfig** *dair kay-fik*	
bowl	**die Schüssel** *dee shews-sel*	
collar	**das Halsband** *duss hulls-bunt*	
lead	**die Leine** *dee lie-ne*	
vet	**der Tierarzt** *dair teer-artst*	
vaccination	**die Impfung** *dee imp-foong*	
pet passport	**der Tierpass** *dair teer-puss*	
fleas	**die Flöhe** *die fler-we*	

5 Put into practice (3 minutes)

Join in this conversation. Read the German on the left and follow the instructions to make your reply. Then test yourself by concealing the answers with the cover flap.

Ist das Ihr Hund?
isst duss eer hoont

Is this your dog?

Say: Yes, he's called Hasso.

Ja, er heißt Hasso.
yah, er hiesst hus-so

Ich habe Angst vor Hunden.
ikh hah-be unkst foer hoon-den

I'm frightened of dogs.

Say: Don't worry, he's well behaved.

Keine Angst, er ist gutartig.
kie-ne unkst, er isst goot-ar-tikh

WIEDERHOLUNG
Review and repeat

1 Colours

❶ **schwarz**
shvarts

❷ **weiß**
vies

❸ **rot**
roet

❹ **grün**
grewn

❺ **gelb**
gelp

1 Colours (4 minutes)

Complete the sentences with the German word for the colour in brackets.

❶ Haben Sie diese Jacke in _____ . (*black*)

❷ Ich nehme den Rock in _____ . (*white*)

❸ Haben Sie die Hose in _____ ? (*red*)

❹ Nein, aber ich habe eine in _____ .
(*green*)

❺ Ich möchte diese Schuhe in _____ .
(*yellow*)

2 Kitchen

❶ **der Herd**
dair hairt

❷ **der Kühlschrank**
dair kewl-shrunk

❸ **das Spülbecken**
duss spewl-bek-ken

❹ **die Mikrowelle**
dee mee-kro-vel-le

❺ **der Backofen**
dair bak-oe-fen

❻ **der Stuhl**
dair shtool

❼ **der Tisch**
dair tish

2 Kitchen (4 minutes)

Say the German words for the numbered items.

cooker ❶   fridge ❷
❺ oven   chair ❻   table ❼

3 House (4 minutes)

You are being shown around a house in Germany.
Join in the conversation, replying in German
following the numbered English prompts.

Hier ist das Wohnzimmer.
❶ What a lovely sofa.

Ja, und da ist auch eine große Küche.
❷ How many rooms?

Es gibt drei Zimmer.
❸ Do you have a garage?

Nein, aber da ist ein großer Garten.
❹ When is the house available?

Ab Juli.
❺ What is the rent per month?

3 House

❶ **Was für eine schöne Couch!**
vuss fewr ie-ne shern-ne kowtch

❷ **Wie viele Zimmer gibt es?**
vee fee-le tsim-mer geept es

❸ **Haben Sie eine Garage?**
hah-ben zee ie-ne ga-ra-je

❹ **Ab wann ist das Haus frei?**
up vunn isst duss hows frie

❺ **Wie hoch ist die monatliche Miete?**
vee hoekh isst dee mo-naht-li-khe mee-te

microwave ❹

❸ sink

4 At home (3 minutes)

Say the German for the following items:

❶ washing machine
❷ sofa
❸ attic
❹ dining room
❺ tree
❻ garden

4 At home

❶ **die Waschmaschine**
dee vush-mah-shee-ne

❷ **die Couch**
dee kowtch

❸ **der Dachboden**
dair dukh-boe-den

❹ **das Esszimmer**
duss es-tsim-mer

❺ **der Baum**
dair bowm

❻ **der Garten**
dair gar-ten

① Warm up (1 minute)

Ask "Where can I find the bank?" (pp.68-9)

What's the German for "passport"? (pp.54-5)

Ask "What time?" (pp.30-1)

BANK UND POST
Bank and post office

German post offices have machines that print stamps on demand, weigh parcels automatically, and explain their services in several languages. Most banks have cash machines (ATMs) with multiple language options. However, banks also offer a cashier service, if you need help.

② Words to remember: post (3 minutes)

der Umschlag *dair oom-shlahk*	envelope
die Postkarte *dee posst-kar-te*	postcard
das Paket *duss pa-kayt*	parcel
per Luftpost *pair looft-posst*	by air mail
per Einschreiben *pair ine-shrie-ben*	by registered post
der Briefkasten *dair breef-kuss-ten*	post box
die Postleitzahl *dee posst-lite-tsahl*	postcode
der Briefträger *dair breef-tray-ger*	postman

Familiarize yourself with these words and test yourself using the cover flap to conceal the German on the left.

die Briefmarken
dee breef-mar-ken
stamps

Wie hoch ist das Porto nach England?
vee hoekh isst duss por-toe nahkh eng-lant
What is the postage for England?

③ In conversation (3 minutes)

Ich möchte Geld abheben.
ikh merkh-te gelt up-hay-ben

I'd like to withdraw some money.

Können Sie sich ausweisen?
kern-nen zee zikh ows-vie-zen

Do you have any ID?

Ja, ich habe meinen Pass dabei.
Yah, ikh hah-be mye-nen puss da-bie

Yes, I have my passport with me.

4 Words to remember: bank (2 minutes)

Familiarize yourself with these words and test yourself using the cover flap.

PIN	**die Geheimnummer**	*dee ge-hime-noom-mer*
bank	**die Bank**	*dee bunk*
cashier	**der Kassierer(in)**	*dair kuss-see-rer(in)*
ATM	**der Geldautomat**	*dair gelt-ow-to-maht*
notes	**die Banknoten**	*dee bunk-noe-ten*
coin	**die Münze**	*dee mewn-tse*
credit card	**die Kreditkarte**	*dee kray-deet-kar-te*

Wie kann ich zahlen?
vee kunn ikh tsah-len
How can I pay?

5 Useful phrases (4 minutes)

Learn these phrases and then test yourself using the cover flap.

I'd like to change some money.	**Ich möchte Geld wechseln.** *ikh merkh-te gelt vek-zeln*
What is the exchange rate?	**Wie ist der Wechselkurs?** *vee isst dair vek-zel-koors*
I'd like to withdraw some money.	**Ich möchte Geld abheben.** *ikh merkh-te gelt up-hay-ben*

6 Say it (2 minutes)

I'd like a stamp.

Where can I find a post box?

I have ID.

Bitte geben Sie Ihre Geheimzahl ein
bit-te gay-ben zee ee-re ge-hime-tsahl ine

Please key in your PIN.

Muss ich auch unterschreiben?
mooss ikh owkh oon-ter-shrie-ben

Do I need to sign as well?

Nein, das ist nicht nötig.
nine, duss isst nikht ner-tikh

No, that's not necessary.

DIENSTLEISTUNGEN
Services

1 **Warm up** (1 minute)

What is the German for "doesn't work"? (pp.60-1)

What's the German for "today" and "tomorrow"? (pp.28-9)

You can combine the German words on these pages with the vocabulary you learned in week 10 to help you explain basic problems and cope with arranging most repairs. When organizing building work or a repair, it's a good idea to agree the price and method of payment in advance.

2 **Words to remember** (4 minutes)

Familiarize yourself with these words and test yourself using the flap.

Klempner(in) *klemp-ner(in)*	plumber
Elektriker(in) *ay-lek-tree-ker(in)*	electrician
Mechaniker(in) *me-khah-nee-ker(in)*	mechanic
Bauarbeiter(in) *bow-ar-bie-ter(in)*	builder
die Putzfrau *dee poots-frow*	cleaning lady
Maler(in) *mah-ler(in)*	painter/decorator
Schreiner(in) *shrie-ner(in)*	carpenter
die Telefonnummer *dee tay-lay-foen-noom-mer*	telephone number

der Radschüssel
dair raht-shlews-sel
wheel brace

Ich brauche keinen Mechaniker.
ikh brow-khe kie-nen me-khah-nee-ke
I don't need a mechanic.

3 **In conversation** (3 minutes)

Die Waschmachine funktioniert nicht.
dee vush-mah-shee-ne foonk-tsee-oen-eert nikht

The washing machine is not working.

Ja, die Pumpe ist kaputt.
yah, dee poom-pe isst ka-poott

Yes, the pipe is broken.

Können Sie die reparieren?
kern-nen zee dee re-pah-ree-ren

Can you repair it?

4 Useful phrases (3 minutes)

Learn these phrases and then test yourself using the cover flap.

Can you clean the bathroom?	**Können Sie das Badezimmer putzen?** *kern-nen zee duss bah-de-tsim-mer poot-tsen*
Can you repair the boiler?	**Können Sie den Boiler reparieren?** *kern-nen zee dayn boi-ler re-pah-ree-ren*
Do you know a good electrician?	**Kennen Sie einen guten Elektriker?** *ken-nen zee ie-nen goo-ten ay-lek-tree-ker*

Wo kann ich das reparieren lassen?
voe kunn ikh duss re-pah-ree-ren luss-sen
Where can I get this repaired?

5 Put into practice (4 minutes)

Learn these phrases. Cover up the text on the right and complete the dialogue in German. Check your answers and repeat if necessary.

Ihr Tor ist kaputt.
eer tohr isst ka-poott

Your gate is broken.

Ask: Do you know a good carpenter?

Kennen Sie einen guten Schreiner?
ken-nen zee ie-nen goo-ten shrie-ner

Ja, es gibt einen im Ort.
yah, es geept ie-nen im ort

Yes, there is one in the village.

Ask: Do you have the telephone number?

Haben Sie die Telefonnummer?
hah-ben zee dee tay-lay-foen-noom-mer

Nein, Sie brauchen eine neue.
nine, zee brow-khen ie-ne noy-e

No, you'll need a new one.

Können Sie das heute machen?
kern-nen zee duss hoy-te ma-khen

Can you do it today?

Nein, ich komme morgen wieder.
nine, ikh kom-me mor-gen vee-der

No. I'll come back tomorrow.

1 **Warm up** (1 minute)

Say the days of the week in German. (pp.28-9)

How do you say "builder"? (pp.110-11)

Say "It's 9.30", "10.45", and "12.00". (pp.10-11, pp.30-1)

KOMMEN
To come

The verb **kommen** (to come) is another important verb. Apart from its literal meaning, it can mean *happen* as in *how come?* It can be combined with adverbs such as **her** (*here*) or **herein** (*in*). It also occurs in many expressions, such as **das kommt davon, dass...** (*That's because...*).

2 **Kommen: to come** (6 minutes)

Say the different forms of **kommen** (to come) aloud. Use the cover flap to test yourself and, when you are confident, practise the sample sentences below.

ich komme *ikh kom-me*	I come
du kommst *doo komst*	you come (informal)
er/sie/es kommt *air/zee/es komt*	he/she/it comes
wir kommen *veer kom-men*	we come
ihr kommt *eer komt*	you come (informal, plural)
sie/Sie kommen *zee kom-men*	they come/you come (plural or formal)
Ich komme aus London. *ikh kom-me ows london*	I come from London.
Wir kommen jeden Dienstag. *veer kom-men yay-den deens-tahk*	We come every Tuesday.
Sie kommen mit dem Zug. *zee kom-men mit daym tsook*	They come by train.

Er kommt aus China.
air komt ows khee-nah
He comes from China.

Conversational tip **Kommen** is used in many (usually friendly) commands such as **komm her** (*come here*) or **kommen Sie herein** (*come in*). It also often appears together with another verb, when in English we might link the two verbs with *and*, as in: **komm setz dich** (*come and sit down*), **kommt essen** (*come and eat*).

3 Useful phrases (4 minutes)

Learn these phrases and then test yourself using the cover flap.

When can I come?	**Wann kann ich kommen?** *vunn kunn ikh kom-men*
Where does she come from?	**Woher kommt sie?** *vo-hair komt zee*
The cleaner comes every Monday.	**Die Putzfrau kommt jeden Montag.** *dee poots-frow komt yay-den moen-tahk*
Come with me. (informal/formal)	**Komm mit/ Kommen Sie mit.** *kom mit/ kom-men zee mit*

Bitte setzen Sie sich.
bit-te zet-sen zee zikh
Come and sit down.

4 Put into practice (4 minutes)

Join in this conversation. Read the German on the left and follow the instructions to make your reply. Then test yourself by concealing the answers with the cover flap.

Guten Tag, Friseursalon Hannelore.
goo-ten tahk, fri-zer-zah-long hun-ne-loe-re

Hello, this is Hannelore's hair salon.

Say: I'd like an appointment.

Ich hätte gern einen Termin.
ikh het-te gairn ie-nen terr-meen

Wann möchten Sie kommen?
vunn merkh-ten zee kom-men

When would you like to come?

Say: Can I come today?

Kann ich heute kommen?
kunn ikh hoy-te kom-men

Natürlich. Um wieviel Uhr?
na-tewr-likh. oomm vee-feel oor

Yes, of course. What time?

Say: At 10.30.

Um halb elf.
oomm hulp elf

1 **Warm up** (1 minute)

What's the German for "big/tall" and "small/short"? (pp.64–5)

Say "The room is big" and "The bed is small". (pp.64–5)

POLIZEI UND VERBRECHEN
Police and crime

*German traffic police (**Verkehrspolizei**) carry out checks and impose fines for violations of the traffic regulations. If you are the victim of a crime or are in a traffic accident in Germany, report it to the nearest police station.*

2 **Words to remember: crime** (4 minutes)

Familiarize yourself with these words.

der Diebstahl *dair deep-shtahl*	robbery
der Polizeibericht *dair po-lee-tsie-be-rikht*	police report
der Dieb *dair deep*	thief
die Polizei *dee po-lee-tsie*	police
die Aussage *dee ows-zah-ge*	statement
Rechtsanwalt/-wältin *rekhts-un-vullt/-vael-tin*	lawyer
Zeuge/Zeugin *tsoy-ge/tsoy-gin*	witness

Ich brauche einen Rechtsanwalt.
ikh brow-khe ie-nen rekhts-un-vullt
I need a lawyer.

3 **Useful phrases** (3 minutes)

Memorize these phrases and then test yourself.

Ich bin bestohlen worden. *ikh bin be-shtoe-len vor-den*	I've been robbed.
Was ist gestohlen worden? *vuss isst ge-shtoe-len vor-den*	What was stolen?
Haben Sie den Täter gesehen? *hah-ben zee den tay-ter ge-zay-en*	Did you see who did it?
Wann ist es passiert? *vunn isst es puss-seert*	When did it happen?

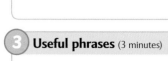

die Wertsachen
dee vairt-zakh-en
valuables

4 Words to remember: appearance (5 minutes)

Learn these words for describing people.

Er hat eine Glatze und einen Bart.
air hut ie-ne glut-se oont ie-nen bart
He is bald and has a beard.

Er hat kurze, schwarze Haare.
air hut koor-tse, shvar-tse hah-re
He has short, black hair.

man	**der Mann**	*dair munn*
woman	**die Frau**	*dee frow*
tall	**groß**	*groes*
short	**klein**	*kline*
young	**jung**	*yoong*
old	**alt**	*ullt*
fat	**dick**	*dick*
thin	**dünn**	*dewnn*
long/short hair	**lange/kurze Haare**	*lun-ge/koor-tse hah-re*
glasses	**die Brille**	*dee bril-le*
beard	**der Bart**	*dair bart*

Cultural tip If you have a car accident or serious breakdown on a motorway, use one of the special telephones that you can find at regular intervals. Elsewhere, phone 112, which is free from all telephones in Germany. The operator will inform the appropriate service (police, fire service, or ambulance) immediately.

5 Put into practice (2 minutes)

Practise these phrases. Then cover up the text on the right and follow the instructions to make your reply in German.

Wie sah er aus? **Klein und dick.**
vee zah air ows *kline oont dick*

What did he look like?

Say: Short and fat.

Und die Haare? **Lang, mit Bart.**
oont dee hah-re *lung, mit bart*

And the hair?

Say: Long, with a beard.

WIEDERHOLUNG
Review and repeat

1 To come

1 komme
kom-me

2 kommt
komt

3 kommen
kom-men

4 kommt
komt

5 kommen
kom-men

1 To come (3 minutes)

Put the correct form of **kommen** (*to come*) into the gaps.

1 Ich _____ um vier Uhr.

2 Der Gärtner _____ einmal in der Woche.

3 Wir _____ Dienstag zum Essen.

4 _____ ihr mit?

5 Meine Eltern _____ mit dem Zug.

2 Bank and post

1 die Banknoten
dee bunk-noe-ten

2 das Paket
duss pa-kayt

3 die Postkarte
dee posst-kar-te

4 die Briefmarken
dee breef-mar-ken

2 Bank and post (4 minutes)

Name the numbered items in German.

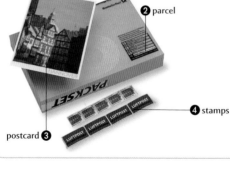

1 notes

2 parcel

3 postcard

4 stamps

Antworten
Answers (Cover with flap)

3 Appearance (4 minutes)

What do these descriptions mean?

❶ Der Mann ist groß und dünn.

❷ Sie hat kurze Haare und eine Brille.

❸ Ich bin klein und habe lange Haare.

❹ Sie ist alt und dick.

❺ Er hat blaue Augen und einen Bart.

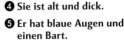

3 Appearance

❶ The man is tall and thin.

❷ She has short hair and glasses.

❸ I'm short and I have long hair.

❹ She is old and fat.

❺ He has blue eyes and a beard.

4 The pharmacy (4 minutes)

You are asking a pharmacist for advice. Join in the conversation, replying in German where you see the numbered English prompts.

Guten Tag, kann ich Ihnen helfen?
❶ I have a cough.

Und haben Sie auch Schnupfen?
❷ No, but I have a headache.

Nehmen Sie diese Tabletten.
❸ Do you have that as a syrup?

Selbstverständlich. Bitte sehr.
❹ Thank you. How much is that?

Sechs Euro.
❺ Here you are. Goodbye.

4 The pharmacy

❶ **Ich habe Husten.**
ikh hah-be hoos-ten

❷ **Nein, aber ich habe Kopfschmerzen.**
nine, ah-ber ikh hah-be kopf-shmairt-sen

❸ **Haben Sie das auch als Sirup?**
hah-ben zee duss owkh ulls zee-roop

❹ **Danke. Was macht das?**
dun-ke. vuss mukht duss

❺ **Bitte sehr. Auf Wiedersehen.**
bit-te zair. owf vee-der-zay-en

DIE FREIZEIT
Leisure time

In Germany the arts, from opera and classic drama to performance art and cabaret, and from great composers to folk and avant-garde music, are keenly followed and receive public support. **Lust haben** is a useful expression, meaning to *like the idea of doing something*.

1 **Warm up** (1 minute)

What is the German for "museum" and "art gallery"? (pp.48–9)

Say "I don't like the curtains". (pp.100–1)

Ask "Do you want...?" informally. (pp.22–3)

2 **Words to remember** (4 minutes)

Familiarize yourself with these words.

das Theater *duss tay-ah-ter*	theatre
das Kino *duss kee-no*	cinema
das Ballett *duss bull-let*	ballet
die Musik *dee moo-zeek*	music
die Kunst *dee koonst*	art
der Sport *dair shport*	sport
die Besichtigungen *dee be-zikh-tee-goong-en*	sightseeing
die Computerspiele *dee com-pyoo-ter-shpee-le*	computer games

Ich liebe Opern.
ikh lee-be oh-pairn
I love opera.

das Publikum
duss poo-blee-koomm
audience

3 **In conversation** (4 minutes)

Hast du Lust, heute Tennis zu spielen?
husst doo loost, hoy-te ten-nis tsoo shpee-len

Do you want to play tennis today?

Nein, ich mag keinen Sport.
nine, ikh mahk kie-nen shport

No, I don't like sport.

Wofür interessierst du dich denn?
voe-fewr in-ter-es-seerst doo dikh den

So what are you interested in?

Ich hasse Gitarrenmusik.
ikh hus-se gee-tar-ren-moo-zeek
I hate guitar music.

der Rang
dair rung
circle

4 Useful phrases (4 minutes)

Learn these phrases and then test yourself using the cover flap.

I like the theatre.	**Ich liebe das Theater.** *ikh lee-be duss tay-ah-ter*
I prefer the cinema.	**Ich ziehe das Kino vor.** *ikh tsee-e duss kee-no for*
I'm interested in art.	**Ich interessiere mich für die Kunst.** *ikh in-ter-es-see-re mikh fewr dee koonst*
What are your (formal/informal) interests?	**Wofür interessierst du dich/interessieren Sie sich?** *vo-fewr in-ter-es-seerst doo dikh/in-ter-es-see-ren zee zikh*
That bores me.	**Das finde ich langweilig.** *duss fin-de ikh lung-vie-likh*

das Parkett
duss par-ket
stalls

5 Say it (2 minutes)

I'm interested in music.

I prefer sport.

I don't like computer games.

Ich mache lieber Besichtigungen.
ikh ma-khe lee-ber be-zikh-tee-goong-en

I prefer sightseeing.

Das interessiert mich nicht.
duss in-ter-es-seert mikh nikht

That doesn't interest me.

Kein Problem. Ich gehe allein.
kine pro-blaym. ikh gay-he ull-line

No problem. I'll go on my own.

SPORT UND HOBBYS
Sport and hobbies

① Warm up (1 minute)

Ask "Do you (informal) want to play tennis?" (pp.118-19)

Say "I like the cinema", "I prefer sightseeing", and "That doesn't interest me". (pp.118-19)

Germany is a nation of sports enthusiasts. Many people cycle, jog, swim, or work out at the gym, and many follow sport as spectators. Football is very popular, but so are boxing, ice hockey, tennis, and skiing. The verb **spielen** (*to play*) is mainly used for ball games.

② Words to remember: sports (5 minutes)

Familiarize yourself with these words and test yourself using the flap.

der Bunker
dair boon-ker
bunker

der Golfspieler
dair golf-shpee-ler
golfer

der Fußball *dair foos-bull*	football
das Boxen *duss box-en*	boxing
das Tennis *duss ten-nis*	tennis
das Schwimmen *duss shvim-men*	swimming
das Segeln *duss zay-geln*	sailing
das Angeln *duss ung-eln*	fishing
das Radfahren *duss raht-fah-ren*	cycling
das Wandern *duss vunn-dairn*	hiking

Ich spiele jeden Tag Golf.
ikh shpee-le yay-den tahk golf
I play golf every day.

③ Useful phrases (2 minutes)

Familiarize yourself with these phrases.

Ich spiele Fußball. *ikh shpee-le foos-bull*	I play football.
Wir spielen gern Tennis. *veer shpee-len gairn ten-nis.*	We like playing tennis.
Sie malt. *zee mahlt.*	She paints.

4 Words to remember: hobbies (4 minutes)

Learn these words and phrases, and then test yourself using the cover flap.

do-it-yourself	**das Basteln** *duss bass-teln*
pottery	**die Töpferei** *dee ter-pfe-rie*
flower arranging	**das Blumenstecken** *duss bloo-men-shtek-en*
gardening	**die Gartenarbeit** *dee gar-ten-ar-biet*
singing	**das Singen** *duss zing-en*
Can I join a club?	**Kann ich einem Klub beitreten?** *kunn ikh ien-em kloop bie-tray-ten*
Do I have to be a member?	**Muss man Mitglied sein?** *moos munn mit-gleet zine*
Can I hire the equipment?	**Kann ich die Ausrüstung mieten?** *kumm ikh dee ows-rews-toong mee-ten*

Ich begesitere mich für das Fotografieren.
ikh be-gesi-tair mikh fewr foe-to-grah-fee-ayren
I'm keen on photography.

die Flagge
dee flug-ge
flag

der Golfplatz
dair golf-pluts
golf course

5 Put into practice (3 minutes)

Join in this conversation. Conceal the text on the right and complete the dialogue in German using the cover flap. Check your answers.

Was machst du gern?
vuss mukhst doo gairn

What do you like doing?

Say: I like playing tennis.

Ich spiele gern Tennis.
ikh shpee-le gairn ten-nis

Spielst du auch Golf?
speelst doo owkh golf

Do you also play golf?

Say: No, I play football.

Nein, ich spiele Fußball.
nine, ikh shpee-le foos-bull

Spielst du oft?
speelst doo oft

Do you play often?

Say: Yes, I play every week.

Ja, ich spiele jede Woche.
yah, ikh shpee-le yay-de vokh-e

BESUCHEN
Socializing

In Germany, much socializing takes place outside the home. People meet up to go to a play, a film, or a sports event together, or they go out for a meal or a drink. Friends and family also invite each other for meals, especially for special occasions such as birthdays.

der Gast
dair gust
guest

② Useful phrases (3 minutes)

Learn these phrases and then test yourself.

Ich möchte Sie zum Abendessen einladen. *ikh merkh-te zee tsoom ah-bent-ess-sen ine-lah-den*	I'd like to invite you for dinner.
Sind Sie nächsten Mittwoch frei? *zint zee nayks-ten mit-vokh frie*	Are you free next Wednesday?
Vielleicht ein andermal. *feel-liekht ine un-der-mahl*	Perhaps another time.

Cultural tip When you go to someone's house for the first time, flowers are a welcome gift. If you are invited again, being better acquainted, you can bring something a little more personal.

③ In conversation (3 minutes)

Möchten Sie zum Mittagessen kommen?
merkh-ten zee tsoom mit-tahk-ess-sen kom-men

Would you like to come to lunch?

Mit Vergnügen. Wann?
mit fer-g-new-gen. vunn

I'd be delighted. When?

Wie wär's mit Donnerstag?
vee vairs mit don-ners-tahk

What about Thursday?

die Gastgeberin
dee gust-gay-be-rin
hostess

4 Words to remember (3 minutes)

Familiarize yourself with these words and test
yourself using the flap.

party	**die Party** *dee par-tee*
dinner party	**das Abendessen** *duss ah-bent-ess-sen*
invitation	**die Einladung** *dee ine-lah-doong*
reception	**der Empfang** *dair emp-fung*
cocktail party	**die Cocktailparty** *dee kock-tayl-par-tee*

5 Put into practice (5 minutes)

Join in this conversation.

Können Sie heute Abend zu einem Empfang kommen?
ker-nen zee hoy-te ah-bent tsoo ie-nem emp-fung kom-men

Can you come to a reception tonight?

Ja, gerne.
yah, gair-ne

Say: Yes, I'd love to.

Danke für die Einladung.
dun-ke fewr dee ine-lah-doonk.
Thank you for inviting us.

Es fängt um zwanzig Uhr an.
es fengt oom tsvun-tsik oor un

It starts at eight o'clock.

Was trägt man?
vuss traygt munn

Ask: What should I wear?

Das passt mir gut.
duss pusst meer goot

That's good for me.

Bringen Sie Ihren Mann mit.
brin-gen zee ee-ren munn mit

Bring your husband.

Danke. Um wieviel Uhr?
dun-ke. oom vee-feel oor

Thank you. At what time?

WIEDERHOLUNG
Review and repeat

1 Animals

❶ **der Fisch**
dair fish

❷ **der Vogel**
dair foh-gel

❸ **der Hamster**
dair hums-ter

❹ **die Katze**
dee kut-se

❺ **das Kaninchen**
duss kah-neen-khen

❻ **der Hund**
dair hoont

1 Animals (3 minutes)

Name the animals.

❶ fish

❷ bird

hamster ❸

❹ cat

2 I like...

❶ **Ich spiele gern Fußball.**
ikh shpee-le gairn foos-bull

❷ **Ich spiele nicht gern Golf.**
ikh shpee-le nikht gairn golf

❸ **Ich male gern.**
ikh mah-le gairn

❹ **Blumenstecken mache ich nicht gern.**
bloo-men-shtek-ken makh-e ikh nikht gairn

2 I like... (4 minutes)

Say the following in German.

❶ I like playing football.
❷ I don't like playing golf.
❸ I like to paint.
❹ I don't like flower arranging.

5 rabbit

6 dog

3 Leisure (4 minutes)

What is the German for these sports and leisure activities?

1 sailing
2 art
3 sightseeing
4 cinema
5 hiking
6 swimming

3 Leisure

1 das Segeln
duss zay-geln

2 die Kunst
dee koonst

3 die Besichtigungen
dee be-zikh-tee-goong-en

4 das Kino
duss kee-no

5 das Wandern
duss vunn-dairn

6 das Schwimmen
duss shvim-men

4 An invitation (4 minutes)

You are invited for dinner. Join in the conversation, replying in German following the English prompts.

Möchten Sie am Freitag zum Essen kommen?
1 I'm sorry, I'm busy.

Wie wär's mit Samstag?
2 I'd be delighted.

Bringen Sie Ihre Kinder mit.
3 Thank you. At what time?

Um halb eins.
4 That's good for me.

4 An invitation

1 Es tut mir Leid, ich habe schon etwas vor.
es toot meer liet, ikh hah-be shoen et-vuss for

2 Mit Vergnügen.
mit fer-g-new-gen

3 Danke. Um wieviel Uhr?
dun-ke. oom vee-feel oor

4 Ja, das passt mir.
yah, duss pusst meer

Reinforce and progress

Regular practice is the key to maintaining and advancing your language skills. In this section you will find a variety of suggestions for reinforcing and extending your knowledge of German. Many involve returning to exercises in the book and using the dictionaries to extend their scope. Go back through the lessons in a different order, mix and match activities to make up your own 15-minute daily programme, or focus on topics that are of particular relevance to your current needs.

1 Warm up (1 minute)

Say "I'm sorry". (pp.32-3)

What is the German for "I'd like an appointment"? (pp.32-3)

Ask "with whom?" in German. (pp.32-3)

Keep warmed up
Re-visit the Warm Up boxes to remind yourself of key words and phrases. Make sure you work your way through all of them on a regular basis.

2 I'd like... (3 minutes)

Say you'd like the following:

cake **1**

2 black tea   coffee **3**

Review and repeat again
Work through a Review and Repeat lesson as a way of reinforcing words and phrases presented in the course. Return to the main lesson for any topic on which you are no longer confident.

Carry on conversing
Re-read the In Conversation panels. Say both parts of the conversation, paying attention to the pronunciation. Where possible, try incorporating new words from the dictionary.

3 In conversation: taxi (2 minutes)

Zum Flughafen, bitte.
tsoom flook-hah-fen, bit-te

The airport, please.

Jawohl, kein Problem.
yah-voel. kine pro-blaym

Yes, no problem.

Können Sie mich bitte hier absetzen?
ker-nen zee mikh bit-te heer up-zet-sen

Can you drop me here, please?

4 Useful phrases (3 minutes)

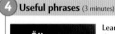

Öffnungszeiten:
Di. - Fr. 11 - 18 Uhr
Sa. + So. 11 - 16 Uhr
(Montags geschlossen)

Learn these phrases and then test yourself using the cover flap.

What time do you open/close?	**Wann öffnen/ schließen Sie?** *vunn erf-nen/shlee-sen zee*
Where are the toilets?	**Wo sind die Toiletten?** *voe zind dee twah-let-ten*
Is there wheelchair access?	**Gibt es Zugang für Rollstuhlfahrer?** *geept es tsoo-gung fewr roll-shtool-fah-rer*

Practise phrases
Return to the Useful Phrases and Put into Practice exercises. Test yourself using the cover flap. When you are confident, devise your own versions of the phrases, using new words from the dictionary.

Match, repeat, and extend
Remind yourself of words related to specific topics by returning to the Match and Repeat and Words to Remember exercises. Test yourself using the cover flap. Discover new words in that area by referring to the dictionary and menu guide.

5 Match and repeat (4 minutes)

Match the numbered items in this scene with the text in the panel.

❶ **der Rhabarber**
dair ra-bar-ber

❷ **die Kartoffeln**
dee kar-toff-eln

❸ **die Radieschen**
dee ra-dees-khen

❹ **der Spinat**
dair shpee-naht

❺ **die Möhren**
dee mer-ren

❻ **der Kohl**
dair koel

❼ **der Lauch**
dair lowk

❽ **der Kohlrabi**
dair koel-rah-bee

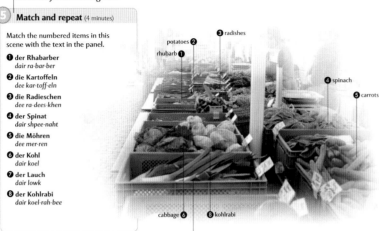

potatoes ❷
rhubarb ❶
❸ radishes
❹ spinach
❺ carrots
cabbage ❻
❽ kohlrabi
❼ leeks

6 Say it (2 minutes)

The lawn needs watering.
Are there any trees?
The gardener comes on Fridays.

Say it again
The Say it exercises are a useful instant reminder for each lesson. Practise these, using your own vocabulary variations from the dictionary or elsewhere in the lesson.

Using other resources

In addition to working with this book, try the following language extension ideas:

Visit a German-speaking country and try out your new skills with native speakers. Find out if there is a German community near you. There may be shops, cafés, restaurants, and clubs. Try to visit some of these and use your German to order food and drink and strike up conversations. Most native speakers will be happy to speak German to you.

Join a language class or club. There are usually evening and day classes available at a variety of different levels. Or you could start a club yourself if you have friends who are also interested in keeping up their German.

Look at German magazines and newspapers. The pictures will help you to understand the text. Advertisements are also a useful way of expanding your vocabulary.

Use the Internet, where you can find all kinds of websites for learning languages, some of which offer free online help and activities. You can also find German websites for anything from renting a house to shampooing your pet. You can even access German radio and TV stations online. Start by going to a German search engine, such as *excite.de*, and keying a subject that interests you, or set yourself a challenge, for example, finding a two-bedroom apartment for rent in Hamburg.

MENU GUIDE

This guide lists the most common terms you may encounter on German menus or when shopping for food. If you can't find an exact phrase, try looking up its component parts.

A

Aal *eel*
am Spieß *on the spit*
Ananas *pineapple*
Äpfel *apple*
Apfel im Schlafrock *baked apple in puff pastry*
Apfelsaft *apple juice*
Apfelsinen *oranges*
Apfelstrudel *apple strudel*
Apfeltasche *apple turnover*
Apfelwein *cider*
Aprikosen *apricots*
Arme Ritter *bread soaked in milk and egg, then fried*
Artischocken *artichokes*
Auberginen *aubergines*
Auflauf *baked pudding or omelette*
Aufschnitt *cold meats*
Austern *oysters*

B

Backobst *dried fruit*
Backpflaume *prune*
Baiser *meringue*
Balkansalat *cabbage and pepper salad*
Bananen *bananas*
Bandnudeln *ribbon noodles*
Basilikum *basil*
Bauernauflauf *bacon and potato omelette*
Bauernfrühstück *fried potato, bacon, and egg*
Bauernomelett *bacon and potato omelette*
Bechamelkartoffeln *potatoes in creamy sauce*
Bedienung *service*
Beilagen *side dishes*
Berliner *jam doughnut*
Bier *beer*
Birnen *pears*
Biskuit *sponge cake*
Bismarckhering *filleted pickled herring*
Blätterteig *puff pastry*
blau *cooked in vinegar; virtually raw (steak)*

Blumenkohl *cauliflower*
blutig *rare*
Blutwurst *black pudding*
Bockwurst *large frankfurter*
Bohnen *beans*
Bouillon *clear soup*
Braten *roast meat*
Brathering *pickled and fried herring, served cold*
Bratkartoffeln *fried potatoes*
Bratwurst *grilled pork sausage*
Brot *bread*
Brötchen *roll*
Brühwurst *large frankfurter*
Brust *breast*
Bückling *smoked red herring*
Buletten *burgers; rissoles*
Bunte Platte *mixed platter*
Burgundersoße *Burgundy wine sauce*
Buttercremetorte *cream cake*
Buttermilch *buttermilk*

C, D

Champignons *mushrooms*
Cordon bleu *veal cordon bleu*
Currywurst mit Pommes frites *curried pork sausage with chips*
Dampfnudeln *sweet yeast dumpling*
Deutsches Beefsteak *minced meat or patty*
Dicke Bohnen *broad beans*
Dillsoße *dill sauce*
durchgebraten *well-done*
durchwachsen *with fat*
durchwachsener Speck *streaky bacon*

E

Eier *eggs*
Eierauflauf *omelette*
Eierkuchen *pancake*
Eierpfannkuchen *egg pancake*
Eierspeise *egg dish*
eingelegt *pickled*
Eintopf *stew*
Eintopfgericht *stew*
Eis *ice*

Eisbecher *sundae*
Eisbein *knuckles of pork*
Eisschokolade *iced chocolate*
Eissplittertorte *ice chip cake*
Endiviensalat *endive salad*
englisch *rare*
Entenbraten *roast duck*
entgrätet *bones (fish)*
Erbsen *peas*
Erdbeertorte *strawberry cake*
Essig *vinegar*

F

Falscher Hase *meat loaf*
Fasan *pheasant*
Fenchel *fennel*
Fett *fat*
Filet *fillet (steak)*
Fisch *fish*
Fischfrikadellen *fishcakes*
Fischstäbchen *fish fingers*
Flädlesuppe *consommé with pancake strips*
flambiert *flambéed*
Fleischbrühe *bouillon*
Fleischkäse *meat loaf*
Fleischklößchen *meatball(s)*
Fleischpastete *meat vol-au-vent*
Fleischsalat *diced meat salad with mayonnaise*
Fleischwurst *pork sausage*
Fond *meat juices*
Forelle *trout*
Forelle Müllerin (Art) *breaded trout with butter and lemon*
Frikadelle *rissole*
Frikassee *fricassee*
fritiert *(deep-) fried*
Froschschenkel *frog's legs*
Fruchtsaft *fruit juice*
Frühlingsrolle *spring roll*

G

Gans *goose*
Gänseleberpastete *goose-liver pâté*
garniert *garnished*
Gebäck *pastries, cakes*
gebacken *baked*
gebraten *roast*

gedünstet *steamed*
Geflügel *poultry*
Geflügelleberragout *chicken liver ragoût*
gefüllt *stuffed*
gefüllte Kalbsbrust *veal roll*
gekocht *boiled*
Gelee *jelly*
gemischter Salat *mixed salad*
Gemüse *vegetable(s)*
Gemüseplatte *assorted vegetables*
gepökelt *salted, pickled*
geräuchert *smoked*
Gericht *dish*
geschmort *braised, stewed*
Geschnetzeltes *strips of fried meat in cream sauce*
gespickt *larded*
Getränke *beverages*
Gewürze *spices*
Gewürzgurken *gherkins*
Goldbarsch *type of perch*
Götterspeise *jelly*
gratiniert *au gratin*
Grieß *semolina*
Grießklößchen *semolina dumplings*
grüne Bohnen *French beans*
grüne Nudeln *green pasta*
grüner Aal *fresh eel*
Grünkohl *(curly) kale*
Gulasch *goulash*
Gulaschsuppe *goulash soup*
Gurkensalat *cucumber salad*

H

Hackfleisch *mince*
Hähnchen *chicken*
Hähnchenkeule *chicken leg*
Haifischflossensuppe *shark-fin soup*
Hammelbraten *roast mutton*
Hammelfleisch *mutton*
Hammelkeule *leg of mutton*
Hammelrücken *saddle of mutton*
Hartkäse *hard cheese*
Haschee *hash*
Hasenkeule *haunch of hare*
Hasenpfeffer *hare casserole*
Hauptspeisen *main courses*
Hecht *pike*
Heidelbeeren *bilberries, blueberries*
Heilbutt *halibut*
Heringsstipp *herring salad*
Heringstopf *pickled herrings in sauce*
Herz *heart*
Herzragout *heart ragoût*
Himbeeren *raspberries*

Himmel und Erde *potato and apple purée with black pudding or liver sausage*
Hirn *brains*
Hirschbraten *roast venison*
Honig *honey*
Honigmelone *honeydew melon*
Hoppelpoppel *bacon and potato omelette*
Hüfte *haunch*
Huhn *chicken*
Hühnerbrühe *chicken broth*
Hühnerfrikassee *chicken fricassee*
Hülsenfrüchte *peas and beans, pulses*
Hummer *lobster*

J, K

Jägerschnitzel *cutlet with mushrooms*
Kabeljau *cod*
Kaffee *coffee*
Kaiserschmarren *sugared pancake with raisins*
Kakao *cocoa*
Kalbfleisch *veal*
Kalbsbries *sweetbread*
Kalbsfrikassee *veal fricassee*
Kalbshaxe *leg of veal*
Kalbsnierenbraten *roast veal with kidney*
Kalbsschnitzel *veal cutlet*
kalte Platte *cold platter*
kaltes Büfett *cold buffet*
Kaltschale *cold, sweet fruit soup*
Kaninchen *rabbit*
Kapern *capers*
Karamelpudding *caramel blancmange*
Karotten *carrots*
Karpfen *carp*
Kartoffelbrei *mashed potato*
Kartoffeln *potatoes*
Kartoffelpuffer *potato fritters*
Kartoffelpüree *mashed potato*
Käse *cheese*
Käsegebäck *cheese savouries*
Käsekuchen *cheesecake*
Käseplatte *selection of cheeses*
Käse-Sahne-Torte *cream cheesecake*
Käsespätzle *home-made noodles with cheese*
Kasseler Rippenspeer *smoked pork loin*
Kasserolle *casserole*
Kassler *smoked pork loin*
Kastanien *chestnuts*
Katenrauchwurst *smoked sausage*
Keule *leg, haunch*
Kieler Sprotten *smoked sprats*

Kirschen *cherries*
klare Brühe *consommé*
Klöße *dumplings*
Knäckebrot *crispbread*
Knacker *spicy fried sausage*
Knackwurst *spicy fried sausage*
Knoblauch *garlic*
Knochen *bone*
Knochenschinken *ham on the bone*
Knödel *dumplings*
Kognak *brandy*
Kohl *cabbage*
Kohlrouladen *stuffed cabbage leaves*
Kohl und Pinkel *cabbage, potatoes, sausage, and smoked meat*
Kompott *stewed fruit*
Konfitüre *jam*
Königinpastete *chicken vol-au-vent*
Königsberger Klopse *meatballs in caper sauce*
Königskuchen *type of fruit cake*
Kopfsalat *lettuce*
Kotelett *chop*
Krabben *shrimps; prawns*
Krabbencocktail *prawn cocktail*
Kraftbrühe *beef consommé*
Kräuter *herbs*
Krautsalat *coleslaw*
Krautwickel *stuffed cabbage leaves*
Krebs *crayfish*
Kresse *cress*
Kroketten *croquettes*
Kruste *crust*
Kuchen *cake*
Kürbis *pumpkin*

L

Labskaus *meat, fish, and potato stew*
Lachs *salmon*
Lachsersatz *sliced, salted pollack (fish)*
Lachsforelle *sea trout*
Lachsschinken *smoked rolled fillet of ham*
Lamm *lamb*
Lammrücken *saddle of lamb*
Langusten *crayfish*
Lauch *leek*
Leber *liver*
Leberkäse *baked pork and beef loaf*
Leberpastete *liver pâté*
Leberwurst *liver pâté*
Lebkuchen *gingerbread*
Leipziger Allerlei *mixed vegetables*
Linsen *lentils*

M

mager *lean*
Majoran *marjoram*
Makrele *mackerel*
Makronen *macaroons*
Mandeln *almonds*
mariniert *marinaded, pickled*
Markklößchen
    marrow dumplings
Marmelade *jam*
Maronen *sweet chestnuts*
Matjes(hering) *young herring*
Medaillons *small fillets*
Meeresfische *seafish*
Meeresfrüchte *seafood*
Meerrettich *horseradish*
Miesmuscheln *mussels*
Milch *milk*
Milchmixgetränk *milk shake*
Milchreis *rice pudding*
Mineralwasser *(sparkling)*
    mineral water
Mohnkuchen *poppyseed cake*
Möhren *carrots*
Mohrrüben *carrots*
Most *fruit wine*
Mus *purée*
Muscheln *mussels*
Muskat(nuss) *nutmeg*
MWSt (Mehrwertsteuer) *VAT*

N, O

nach Art des Hauses
    of the house
nach Hausfrauenart
    home-made
Nachspeisen *desserts*
Nachtisch *dessert*
Napfkuchen *ring-shaped*
    poundcake
natürlich *natural*
Nieren *kidneys*
Nudeln *pasta, noodles*
Nüsse *nuts*
Obstsalat *fruit salad*
Ochsenschwanzsuppe
    oxtail soup
Öl *oil*
Oliven *olives*
Orangen *oranges*
Orangensaft *orange juice*

P

Palatschinken *stuffed pancakes*
paniert *with breadcrumbs*
Paprika *peppers*
Paprikaschoten *peppers*
Paradiesäpfel *tomatoes*
Pastete *vol-au-vent*
Pellkartoffeln *potatoes boiled*
    in their jackets

Petersilie *parsley*
Pfannkuchen *pancake(s)*
Pfeffer *pepper*
Pfifferlinge *chanterelles*
Pfirsiche *peaches*
Pflaumen *plums*
Pflaumenkuchen *plum tart*
Pflaumenmus *plum jam*
Pichelsteiner Topf *vegetable*
    stew with beef
pikant *spicy*
Pilze *mushrooms*
Platte *selection*
pochiert *poached*
Pökelfleisch *salt meat*
Pommes frites
    French fried potatoes
Porree *leek*
Potthast *braised beef*
    with sauce
Poularde *young chicken*
Preiselbeeren *cranberries*
Presskopf *brawn*
Pumpernickel *black rye bread*
Püree *mashed potato*
püriert *puréed*
Putenschenkel *turkey leg*
Puter *turkey*

Q, R

Quark *curd cheese*
Radieschen *radishes*
Rahm *(sour) cream*
Räucheraal *smoked eel*
Räucherhering *kipper,*
    smoked herring
Räucherlachs *smoked salmon*
Räucherspeck *smoked bacon*
Rauchfleisch *smoked meat*
Rehbraten *roast venison*
Rehgulasch *venison goulash*
Rehkeule *haunch of venison*
Rehrücken *saddle of venison*
Reibekuchen *potato waffles*
Reis *rice*
Reisbrei *creamed rice*
Reisrand *with rice*
Remoulade *mayonnaise*
    flavoured with herbs, mustard,
    and capers
Renke *whitefish*
Rettich *radish*
Rhabarber *rhubarb*
Rheinischer Sauerbraten
    roast pickled beef
Rinderbraten *pot roast*
Rinderfilet *fillet steak*
Rinderrouladen *beef olives*
Rinderzunge *ox tongue*
Rindfleisch *beef*
Rippchen *spareribs*
Risi-Pisi *rice and peas*
roh *raw*

Rohkostplatte *selection*
    of salads
Rollmops *rolled-up pickled*
    herring, rollmops
rosa *rare to medium*
Rosenkohl *Brussels sprouts*
Rosinen *raisins*
Rostbraten *roast*
Rostbratwurst
    barbecued sausage
Rösti *fried potatoes*
    and onions
Röstkartoffeln *fried potatoes*
Rotbarsch *type of perch*
Rote Bete *beetroot*
rote Grütze *red fruit jelly*
Rotkohl *red cabbage*
Rotkraut *red cabbage*
Rotwein *red wine*
Rühreier *scrambled eggs*
Russische Eier
    egg mayonnaise

S

Sahne *cream*
Salate *salads*
Salatplatte *selection of salads*
Salatsoße *salad dressing*
Salz *salt*
Salzburger Nockerln
    sweet soufflés
Salzheringe *salted herrings*
Salzkartoffeln *boiled potatoes*
Salzkruste *salty crusted skin*
Sandkuchen *type of*
    Madeira cake
sauer *sour*
Sauerbraten *roast pickled beef*
Sauerkraut *pickled white*
    cabbage
Sauerrahm *sour cream*
Schaschlik *(shish-)kebab*
Schattenmorellen
    morello cherries
Schellfisch *haddock*
Schildkrötensuppe *real*
    turtle soup
Schillerlocken *smoked*
    haddock rolls
Schinken *ham*
Schinkenröllchen *rolled ham*
Schlachtplatte *selection of*
    fresh sausages
Schlagsahne *whipped cream*
Schlei *tench*
Schmorbraten *pot roast*
Schnecken *snails*
Schnittlauch *chives*
Schnitzel *breaded escalope*
Schokolade *chocolate*
Scholle *plaice*
Schulterstück *slice of shoulder*
Schwarzbrot *brown rye bread*

Schwarzwälder Kirschtorte
Black Forest cherry gâteau
Schwarzwurzeln *salsify*
Schwein *pork*
Schweinebauch *belly of pork*
Schweinefleisch *pork*
Schweinerippe *cured pork chop*
Schweinerollbraten *rolled roast of pork*
Schweineschmorbraten
roast pork
Schweineschnitzel *breaded pork cutlet*
Schweinshaxe *knuckle of pork*
Seelachs *pollack (fish)*
Seezunge *sole*
Sekt *sparkling wine*
Sellerie *celeriac*
Semmel *bread roll*
Senf *mustard*
Senfsahnesoße *mustard and cream sauce*
Senfsoße *mustard sauce*
Serbisches Reisfleisch
diced pork, onions, tomatoes, and rice
Soleier *pickled eggs*
Soße *sauce, gravy*
Soufflé *soufflé*
Spanferkel *suckling pig*
Spargel *asparagus*
Spätzle *home-made noodles*
Speck *fatty bacon*
Speisekarte *menu*
Spezialität des Hauses
house speciality
Spiegeleier *fried eggs*
Spießbraten *joint roasted on a spit*
Spinat *spinach*
Spitzkohl *white cabbage*
Sprotten *sprats*
Sprudel(wasser) *mineral water*
Stachelbeeren *gooseberries*
Stangen(weiß)brot
French bread
Steinbutt *turbot*
Steinpilze *cep mushrooms*
Stollen *Christmas fruit loaf*
Strammer Max *ham and fried egg on bread*
Streuselkuchen *cake with crumble topping*
Sülze *brawn*
Suppen *soups*
Suppengrün *mixed herbs and vegetables (used in soup)*
süß *sweet*
süß-sauer *sweet-and-sour*
Süßspeisen *sweet dishes*
Süßwasserfische
freshwater fish
Szegediner Gulasch *goulash with pickled cabbage*

T

Tafelwasser *(still) mineral water*
Tafelwein *table wine*
Tagesgericht *dish of the day*
Tageskarte *menu of the day*
Tagessuppe *soup of the day*
Tatar *steak tartare*
Taube *pigeon*
Tee *tea*
Teigmantel *pastry case*
Thunfisch *tuna*
Tintenfisch *squid*
Tomaten *tomatoes*
Törtchen *tart(s)*
Torte *gâteau*
Truthahn *turkey*

U, V

überbacken *au gratin*
Ungarischer Gulasch
Hungarian goulash
ungebraten *not fried*
Vanille *vanilla*
Vanillesoße *vanilla sauce*
verlorene Eier *poached eggs*
Vollkornbrot *dark whole grain bread*
vom Grill *grilled*
vom Kalb *veal*
vom Rind *beef*
vom Rost *grilled*
vom Schwein *pork*
Vorspeisen *hors d'oeuvres, starters*

W

Waffeln *waffles*
Waldorfsalat *salad with celery, apples, and walnuts*
Wasser *water*
Wassermelone *watermelon*
Weichkäse *soft cheese*
Weinbergschnecken *snails*
Weinbrand *brandy*
Weincreme *pudding with wine*
Weinschaumcreme *creamed pudding with wine*
Weinsoße *wine sauce*
Weintrauben *grapes*
Weißbier *wheat beer*
Weißbrot *white bread*
Weißkohl *white cabbage*
Weißkraut *white cabbage*
Weißwein *white wine*
Weißwurst *veal sausage*
Weizenbier *fizzy, light-coloured beer made with wheat*
Wiener Schnitzel *veal in breadcrumbs*
Wild *game*

Wildschweinkeule *haunch of wild boar*
Wildschweinsteak
wild boar steak
Windbeutel *cream puff*
Wirsing *savoy cabbage*
Wurst *sausage*
Würstchen *frankfurter(s)*
Wurstplatte *selection of sausages*
Wurstsalat *sausage salad*
Wurstsülze *sausage brawn*
würzig *spicy*

Z

Zander *pike-perch, zander*
Zigeunerschnitzel *veal with peppers and relishes*
Zitrone *lemon*
Zitronencreme *lemon cream*
Zucchini *courgettes*
Zucker *sugar*
Zuckererbsen *mangetout*
Zunge *tongue*
Zungenragout *tongue ragoût*
Zutaten *ingredients*
Zwiebeln *onions*
Zwiebelringe *onion rings*
Zwiebelsuppe *onion soup*
Zwiebeltorte *onion tart*
Zwischengerichte *entrées*

DICTIONARY
English to German

In German, the gender of a noun is indicated by the word for *the*: **der** for a masculine noun, **die** for feminine, and **das** for neuter. **Die** is also used with plural nouns, and the abbreviations *m pl*, *f pl*, and *nt pl* are used to indicate their gender here. The feminine form of most occupations and personal attributes is made by adding **-in** to the masculine form: *accountant* **Buchhalter(in)**, for example. Exceptions to this rule are listed separately. Where necessary, adjectives are denoted by the abbreviation *adj*.

A

about: about 16 **etwa 16**
accelerator **das Gaspedal**
accident **der Unfall**
accommodation **die Unterkunft**
accountant **der/die Buchhalter(in)**
ache **der Schmerz**
adaptor **der Adapter**
address **die Adresse**
admission charge **der Eintrittspreis**
after **nach**
aftershave **das Rasierwasser**
again **nochmal**
against **gegen**
agenda **die Tagesordnung**
agent **der Vertreter**
air **die Luft**
air conditioning **die Klimaanlage**
aircraft **das Flugzeug**
airline **die Fluglinie**
airmail **die Luftpost**
air mattress **die Luftmatratze**
airport **der Flughafen**
airport bus **der Flughafenbus**
aisle **der Gang**
alarm clock **der Wecker**
alcohol **der Alkohol**
all **alle(s)**; all the streets **alle Straßen**; that's all **das ist alles**
allergic **allergisch**
almost **fast**
alone **allein**
already **schon**
always **immer**
am: I am **ich bin**
ambulance **der Krankenwagen**
America **Amerika**
American **der/die Amerikaner(in)**; (adj) **amerikanisch**
and **und**
ankle **der Knöchel**

another (different) **ein anderer**; (one more) **noch ein**; another time **ein andermal**; another room **ein anderes Zimmer**; another coffee, please **noch einen Kaffee, bitte**
answering machine **der Anrufbeantworter**
antique shop **das Antiquitätengeschäft**
antiseptic **das Antiseptikum**
apartment **die Wohnung**
aperitif **der Aperitif**
appetite **der Appetit**
apple **der Apfel**
application form **das Antragsformular**
appointment **der Termin**
apricot **die Aprikose**
are: you are (singular informal) **du bist**; (singular formal; plural formal) **sie sind**; (plural informal) **ihr seit**; we are **wir sind**; they are **sie sind**
arm **der Arm**
armchair **der Sessel**
arrivals **die Ankunft**
art **die Kunst**
art gallery **die Kunstgalerie**
artist **der/die Künstler(in)**
as: as soon as possible **so bald wie möglich**
ashtray **der Aschenbecher**
asthma **das Asthma**
at: at the post office **auf der Post**; at the station **am Bahnhof**; at night **in der Nacht**; at 3 o'clock **um 3 Uhr**
ATM **der Geldautomat**
attic **der Dachboden**
attractive **attraktiv**
August **August**
aunt **die Tante**
Australia **Australien**

Australian **der/die Australier(in)**; (adj) **australisch**
Austria **Österreich**
Austrian **der/die Österreicher(in)**; (adj) **österreichisch**
automatic **automatisch**
away: is it far away? **ist es weit von hier?**; go away! **gehen sie weg!**
awful **furchtbar**

B

baby **das Baby**
back (not front) **die Rückseite**; (part of body) **der Rücken**
bacon **der Speck**; bacon and eggs **Eier mit Speck**
bad **schlecht**
bag **die Tasche**
baggage **das Gepäck**; baggage claim **die Gepäckausgabe**
bait **der Köder**
bake **backen**
baker **der Bäcker**
bakery **die Bäckerei**
balcony **der Balkon**
ball **der Ball**
ballet **das Ballett**
Baltic **die Ostsee**
banana **die Banane**
band (musicians) **die Band**
bandage **der Verband**
bank **die Bank**
banknote **der (Geld)schein**
bar (drinks) **die Bar**
barbecue **der Grill**
barber's **der Herrenfriseur**
bargain **das Sonderangebot**
basement **das Untergeschoss**
basin (sink) **das Becken**
basket **der Korb**
bath **das Bad**; (tub) **die Badewanne**; to have a bath **ein Bad nehmen**

bathroom **das Badezimmer**
bathtub **die Badewanne**
battery **die Batterie**
Bavaria **Bayern**
beach **der Strand**
beans **die Bohnen**
beard **der Bart**
beautiful **schön**
because **weil**
bed **das Bett;** *bed linen*
    die Bettwäsche
bedroom **das Schlafzimmer**
bedside table **der Nachttisch**
bedspread **die Tagesdecke**
beef **das Rindfleisch**
beer **das Bier**
before... **vor...**
beginner **der Anfänger**
behind... **hinter...**
beige **beige**
Belgian **der/die Belgier(in);**
    (adj) **belgisch**
Belgium **Belgien**
bell (church) **die Glocke;**
    (door) **die Klingel**
below... **unter...**
belt **der Gürtel**
beside **neben**
best **bester**
better **besser**
between... **zwischen...**
bicycle **das Fahrrad**
big **groß**
bikini **der Bikini**
bill **die Rechnung**
bin liner **der Müllsack**
biochemistry **die Biochemie**
bird **der Vogel**
birthday **der Geburtstag;**
    happy birthday! **Herzlichen**
    Glückwunsch!
birthday card **die**
    Geburtstagskarte
birthday present **das**
    Geburtstagsgeschenk
biscuit **das Keks**
bite (by dog) **der Biss;**
    (by insect) **der Stich;**
    (verb: by dog) **beißen;**
    (by insect) **stechen**
bitter **bitter**
black **schwarz**
blackberry **die Brombeere**
blackcurrant **die schwarze**
    Johannisbeere
Black Forest **der Schwarzwald**
blanket **die Decke**
bleach **das Bleichmittel;**
    (verb: hair) **bleichen**
blind (unsighted) **blind**
blinds **die Jalousie**

blister **die Blase**
blond (adj) **blond**
blood **das Blut;** *blood test*
    die Blutprobe
blouse **die Bluse**
blue **blau**
boarding pass **die Bordkarte**
boat **das Schiff;**
    (small) **das Boot**
body **der Körper;**
    (corpse) **die Leiche**
boil (verb) **kochen**
boiled **gekocht**
boiler **der Boiler**
bolt (on door) **der Riegel;**
    (verb) **verriegeln**
bone **der Knochen**
bonnet (car) **die Motorhaube**
book **das Buch;** (verb) **buchen**
bookshop **die Buchhandlung**
boot (car) **der Kofferraum;**
    (footwear) **der Stiefel**
border **die Grenze**
boring **langweilig**
born: I was born in...
    ich bin in... geboren
both **beide;** *both of us*
    wir beide; *both... and...*
    sowohl... als auch...
bottle **die Flasche**
bottle opener **der**
    Flaschenöffner
bottom **der Boden;**
    (sea) **der Grund**
bowl **die Schüssel**
box **die Schachtel**
boxing **das Boxen**
box office **die Kasse**
boy **der Junge**
boyfriend **der Freund**
bra **der Büstenhalter**
bracelet **das Armband**
braces **die Hosenträger** (nt pl)
brake **die Bremse;**
    (verb) **bremsen**
branch **die Zweigstelle**
brandy **der Weinbrand**
bread **das Brot**
breakdown (car) **die Panne**
breakfast **das Frühstück**
breathe **atmen**
bridge **die Brücke;** (game)
    das Bridge
briefcase **die Aktentasche**
Britain **Großbritannien**
British **britisch**
brochure **die Broschüre**
broken (arm, etc.) **gebrochen;**
    (vase, etc.) **zerbrochen;**
    (machine, etc.) **kaputt;**
    broken leg **der Beinbruch**

brooch **die Brosche**
brother **der Bruder**
brother-in-law **der Schwager**
brown **braun**
bruise **der blaue Fleck**
brush **die Bürste;** (paint)
    der Pinsel; (verb: hair)
    bürsten; (floor) **kehren**
Brussels **Brüssel**
bucket **der Eimer**
budget **das Budget**
builder **der Bauarbeiter(in)**
building **das Gebäude**
bumper **die Stoßstange**
burglar **der Einbrecher**
burn **die Verbrennung;**
    (verb) **brennen**
bus **der Bus;** *bus station*
    der Busbahnhof
business **das Geschäft;**
    it's none of your business
    das geht Sie nichts an
business card **die Visitenkarte**
busy (occupied) **beschäftigt;**
    (bar, etc.) **voll**
but **aber**
butcher's **die Metzgerei**
butter **die Butter**
button **der Knopf**
buy **kaufen**
by: by the window **am Fenster;**
    by Friday **bis Freitag**

C

cabbage **der Kohl**
cable car **die Drahtseilbahn**
café **das Café**
cage **der Käfig**
cake **der Kuchen**
cake shop **die Konditorei**
calculator **der Rechner**
call: what's it called?
    wie heißt das?
camera **die Kamera**
camper van **das Wohnmobil**
campfire **das Lagerfeuer**
camping gas **das Campinggas**
campsite **der Campingplatz;**
    campsite office **die**
    Campingplatzverwaltung
camshaft **die Nockenwelle**
can (vessel) **die Dose;**
    (verb: to be able) *can I*
    have...? **kann ich...haben?;**
    can you...? **können Sie...?**
Canada **Kanada**
Canadian **der/die Kanadier(in);**
    (adj) **kanadisch**
canal **der Kanal**
candle **die Kerze**

canoe das Kanu
cap (bottle) der Verschluss;
(hat) die Mütze
car das Auto
caravan der Wohnwagen
carburettor der Vergaser
card die Karte
careful sorgfältig; be careful!
passen Sie auf!
caretaker der/die
Hausmeister(in)
car park der Parkplatz
carpenter der/die Schreiner(in)
carpet der Teppich
car repairs die Werkstatt
carriage (train) der Wagen
carrot die Möhre, die Karotte
car seat (for baby) der Kindersitz
case (suitcase) der Koffer
cash das Bargeld; (verb)
einlösen; to pay cash
bar bezahlen
cashier der/die Kassierer(in)
cash machine der Geldautomat
cassette die Kassette; cassette
player der Kassettenrecorder
castle das Schloss, die Burg
cat die Katze
cathedral der Dom
cauliflower der Blumenkohl
cave die Höhle
ceiling die Decke
cellar der Keller
cemetery der Friedhof
central heating die
Zentralheizung
centre (middle) die Mitte
certificate die Bescheinigung
chair der Stuhl
change (money) das Kleingeld;
(verb: money) wechseln;
(clothes) sich umziehen
Channel der Kanal; Channel
Tunnel der Kanaltunnel
charger das Ladegerät
cheap billig
check in (desk) der
Abfertigungsschalter,
die Abfertigung;
(verb) einchecken
checkout die Kasse
cheers! prost!
cheese der Käse
chemist's (shop) die Apotheke
cheque der Scheck;
cheque card die Scheckkarte;
chequebook das Scheckheft
cherry die Kirsche
chess Schach
chest (part of body) die Brust;
(furniture) die Truhe

chest of drawers die Kommode
chewing gum der Kaugummi
chicken das Huhn;
(cooked) das Hähnchen
child das Kind
children die Kinder (nt pl)
children's ward die
Kinderstation
chimney der Schornstein
china das Porzellan
chips die Fritten, die Pommes
(m pl)
chocolate die Schokolade;
box of chocolates die
Schachtel Pralinen
chop (food) das Kotelett; (verb:
to cut) kleinschneiden
Christmas Weihnachten
church die Kirche
cigar die Zigarre; (thin)
das Zigarillo
cigarette die Zigarette
cinema das Kino
circle der Rang
city die (Groß)stadt; city centre
das Stadtzentrum
class die Klasse
classical music die
klassische Musik
clean (adj) sauber
cleaner die Putzfrau
clear klar
clever klug
client der Kunde
clock die Uhr
close (near) nah; (stuffy) stickig;
(verb) schließen
closed geschlossen
clothes die Kleider (nt pl)
club der Klub
clubs (cards) Kreuz
clutch die Kupplung
coach der Überlandbus, der
Reisebus; (train) der Wagen;
coach station der Busbahnhof
coat der Mantel
coat hanger der (Kleider)bügel
coffee der Kaffee; black coffee
der Kaffee ohne Milch
coin die Münze
cold (illness) die Erkältung;
(adj) kalt; I have a cold
ich bin erkältet; I am cold
mir ist kalt
collar das Halsband,
der Kragen
collection (stamps, etc.)
die Sammlung;
(postal) die Leerung
Cologne Köln
colour die Farbe;

colour film der Farbfilm
comb der Kamm
come kommen; I come from...
ich komme aus...;
come here! kommen Sie her!
come back zurückkommen
compact disc die Compact-Disc,
die CD
compartment das Abteil
complicated kompliziert
computer der Computer;
computer games die
Computerspiele (nt pl)
concert das Konzert
conditioner (hair) die
Haarspülung
condom das Kondom
conductor (bus) der Schaffner;
(orchestra) der Dirigent
conference die Konferenz;
conference room das
Konferenzzimmer
congratulations! herzlichen
Glückwunsch!
consulate das Konsulat
consultant der/die Berater(in)
contact lenses die Kontaktlinsen
contraceptive das
Verhütungsmittel
contract der Vertrag
cook der Koch; (verb) kochen
cooker der Herd
cool kühl
cork der Korken
corkscrew der Korkenzieher
corner die Ecke
corridor der Korridor
cosmetics die Kosmetika
cost (verb) kosten; what does
it cost? was kostet das?
cot das Kinderbett
cotton die Baumwolle
cotton wool die Watte
cough der Husten;
(verb) husten
country das Land
cousin (male) der Vetter;
(female) die Kusine
crab die Krabbe
cramp der Krampf
crayfish der Krebs
cream (for cake, etc.) die Sahne;
(lotion) die Creme
credit card die Kreditkarte
crisps die Chips
crowded überfüllt
cruise die Kreuzfahrt
crutches die Krücken (f pl)
cry (weep) weinen;
(shout) rufen
cucumber die Gurke

cufflinks die
 Manschettenknöpfe (m pl)
cup die Tasse
cupboard der Schrank
curls die Locken (f pl)
curry das Curry
curtain der Vorhang
cushion das Kissen
Customs der Zoll
cut der Schnitt;
 (verb) schneiden
cycling das Radfahren

D

dad der Papa
dairy products die
 Molkereiprodukte (nt pl)
damp feucht
dance der Tanz; (verb) tanzen
Dane (man) der Däne; (woman)
 die Dänin
dangerous gefährlich
Danish dänisch
Danish pastry das Teilchen
Danube die Donau
dark dunkel
daughter die Tochter
day der Tag
dead tot
deaf taub
dear (person) lieb;
 (expensive) teuer
December Dezember
deck chair der Liegestuhl
decorator der/die Maler(in)
deep tief
delayed verspätet
delegate der/die Delegierte(r)
deliberately absichtlich
delicatessen das
 Feinkostgeschäft
delivery die Lieferung
Denmark Dänemark
dentist der Zahnarzt
dentures die Prothese,
 das Gebiss
deny bestreiten
deodorant das Deodorant
department die Abteilung
department store das Kaufhaus
departure die Abfahrt
departure lounge die Abflughalle
departures der Abflug
deposit die Kaution
designer der/die Grafiker(in)
desserts der Nachtisch
develop (film) entwickeln
diabetic der/die Diabetiker(in)
diamond (gem) der Diamant
diamonds (cards) Karo

diarrhoea der Durchfall
diary das Tagebuch
dictionary das Wörterbuch
die sterben
diesel der Diesel
different verschieden;
 that's different! das ist etwas
 anderes!; *I'd like a different
 kind* ich möchte gern eine
 andere Sorte
difficult schwierig
dining room der Speiseraum
dinner das Abendessen
directory (telephone)
 das Telefonbuch
dirty schmutzig
disabled behindert
discounts die
 Ermäßigungen
dishwasher die
 Geschirrspülmaschine
disposable nappies die
 Einwegwindeln
dive der Sprung;
 (verb) tauchen
diving board das Sprungbett
divorced geschieden
DIY das Basteln
do tun; *how do you do?*
 guten Tag; (on being
 introduced) freut mich
doctor der Arzt
document das Dokument
dog der Hund
doll die Puppe
dollar der Dollar
door die Tür
double room das
 Doppelzimmer
doughnut der Berliner
down herunter; (position)
 unten; *down here* hier unten
drawer die Schublade
drawing pin die Heftzwecke,
 der Reißnagel
dress das Kleid
drink das Getränk; (verb)
 trinken; *would you like
 a drink?* möchten Sie
 etwas trinken?
drinking water das Trinkwasser
drive (verb) fahren
driver der/die Fahrer(in)
driveway die Einfahrt
driving licence der Führerschein
drops die Tropfen
drunk betrunken
dry trocken
dry cleaner die Reinigung
dummy (for baby) der Schnuller
during während

dustbin die Mülltonne
duster das Staubtuch
Dutch (adj) holländisch
Dutchman/woman der/die
 Holländer(in)
duty-free zollfrei
duvet die Steppdecke

E

each (every) jeder, alle; *five euros
 each* fünf Euro das Stück
ear das Ohr; *ears* die
 Ohren (nt pl)
early früh
earrings die Ohrringe (m pl)
east der Osten
easy leicht
eat essen
egg das Ei
eight acht
eighteen achtzehn
eighty achtzig
either: either of them einer
 von beiden; *either... or...*
 entweder... oder...
elastic elastisch; *elastic band*
 das Gummiband
elbow der Ellbogen
electric elektrisch
electrical hook-up der
 Stromanschluss
electrician der/die
 Elektriker(in)
electricity der Strom
eleven elf
else: something else etwas
 anderes; *someone else*
 jemand anders; *somewhere
 else* woanders
e-mail die Mail
e-mail address die Mail Adresse
embarrassing peinlich
embassy die Botschaft
emerald der Smaragd
emergency der Notfall
emergency brake
 die Notbremse
emergency department
 die Unfallstation
emergency exit der
 Notausgang
empty leer
end das Ende
engaged (couple) verlobt;
 (occupied) besetzt
engine (motor) der Motor
engineering die Technik
England England
English (adj) englisch;
 (language) Englisch

Englishman/woman der/die
    Engländer(in)
enlargement die **Vergrößerung**
enough **genug**
entertainment die **Unterhaltung**
entrance der **Eingang**; *entrance
    ticket* die **Eintrittskarte**
envelope der **(Brief)umschlag**
epileptic der/die **Epilektiker(in)**
escalator die **Rolltreppe**
especially **besonders**
estimate der
    Kostenvoranschlag
evening der **Abend**
every **jeder**
everyone **jeder**
everything **alles**
everywhere **überall**
example das **Beispiel**; *for
    example* **zum Beispiel**
excellent **ausgezeichnet**
excess baggage das **Mehrgepäck**
exchange (verb) **(um)tauschen**
exchange rate der **Wechselkurs**
excursion der **Ausflug**
excuse me! **Entschuldigung!**
executive der/die **Manager(in)**
exhaust der **Auspuff**
exhibition die **Ausstellung**
exit der **Ausgang**
expensive **teuer**
extension lead die
    Verlängerungsschnur
eye das **Auge**;
    eyes die **Augen**
eyebrow das **Augenbraue**

F

face das **Gesicht**
faint (unclear) **blass**; (verb)
    ohnmächtig werden
fair (funfair) der **Jahrmarkt**, die
    Kirmes; (just) **gerecht, fair**
false teeth die **Prothese**,
    das **Gebiss**
family die **Familie**
fan (ventilator) der **Ventilator**;
    (enthusiast) der **Fan**
fan belt der **Keilriemen**
fantastic **fantastisch**
far **weit**; *how far is it?*
    wie weit ist es?
fare der **Fahrpreis**
farm der **Bauernhof**
farmer der **Bauer**
fashion die **Mode**
fast **schnell**
fat das **Fett**; (person) **dick**
father der **Vater**

February **Februar**
feel (touch) **fühlen**; *I feel hot*
    mir ist heiß; *I feel like...*
    ich möchte gern...; *I don't
    feel well* **mir ist nicht gut**
feet die **Füße** (m pl)
fence der **Zaun**
ferry die **Fähre**
fever das **Fieber**
fiancé der **Verlobte**
fiancée die **Verlobte**
field das **Feld**; (of work)
    das **Gebiet**
fifteen **fünfzehn**
fifty **fünfzig**
fig die **Feige**
filling (in tooth, cake) die **Füllung**;
    (in sandwich) der **Belag**
film der **Film**
filter der **Filter**
filter papers das **Filterpapier**
finger der **Finger**
fire das **Feuer**
fire extinguisher der
    Feuerlöscher
fireworks das **Feuerwerk**
first **erster**; *first class*
    erster Klasse
first aid die **Erste Hilfe**
first floor der **erste Stock**
first name der **Vorname**
fish der **Fisch**
fishing das **Angeln**; *to go fishing*
    Angeln gehen
fishmonger's das **Fischgeschäft**
five **fünf**
fizzy **sprudelnd**
fizzy water **Wasser mit
    Kohlensäure, das
    Sprudelwasser**
flag die **Fahne**
flash (camera) der **Blitz**
flat (level) **flach**;
    (apartment) die **Wohnung**
flat tyre der **Platten**
flavour der **Geschmack**
flea der **Floh**
flea spray das **Flohspray**
flight der **Flug**; *flight number*
    die **Flugnummer**
flippers die
    (Schwimm)flossen (f pl)
floor (ground) der **Fußboden**,
    der **Boden**; (storey)
    der **Stock**
florist der **Blumenladen**
flour das **Mehl**
flower die **Blume**;
    flower-arranging das
    Blumenstecken;
    flowerbed das **Blumenbeet**

flute die **Flöte**
fly (insect) die **Fliege**;
    (verb) **fliegen**
flyover die **Überführung**
fly sheet das **Überzelt**
fog der **Nebel**
folk music die **Volksmusik**
food das **Essen**
food poisoning die
    Lebensmittelvergiftung
foot der **Fuß**
football der **Fußball**
for **für**; *for me* **für mich**;
    what for? **wofür?**; *for a week*
    für eine Woche
foreigner der/die
    Ausländer(in)
forest der **Wald**
forget **vergessen**
fork die **Gabel**
fortnight **zwei Wochen**
forty **vierzig**
fountain der **Brunnen**
four **vier**
fourteen **vierzehn**
fourth **vierter**
France **Frankreich**
free **frei**; (no charge) **kostenlos,
    gratis**
freezer der **Gefrierschrank**
French **französisch**
Frenchman der **Franzose**
Frenchwoman die **Französin**
Friday **Freitag**
fridge der **Kühlschrank**
fried **gebraten**
friend der/die **Freund(in)**
friendly **freundlich**
front: in front of... **vor...**
frost der **Frost**
frozen foods die **Tiefkühlkost**
fruit das **Obst**, die **Frucht**
fruit juice der **Fruchtsaft**
fry **braten**
frying pan die **(Brat)pfanne**
full **voll**; *I'm full (up)*
    ich bin satt
full board **Vollpension**
funny **komisch**
furniture die **Möbel**

G

garage die **Garage**;
    (for repairs) die **Werkstatt**
garden der **Garten**
garden centre das **Gartencenter**
gardener der/die **Gärtner(in)**
gardening die **Gartenarbeit**
garlic der **Knoblauch**
gate das **Tor**; (garden gate)

die Pforte; (at airport)
der Flugsteig
gay (homosexual) **schwul**
gear **der Gang**
gearbox **das Getriebe**
gear stick **der Schaltknüppel**
gel (hair) **das Gel**
German **der/die Deutsche**;
(adj) **deutsch**;
(language) **Deutsch**
Germany **Deutschland**
get (fetch) **holen**; *have you got...?*
haben Sie...?; *to get the train*
den Zug nehmen
get back: we get back tomorrow
wir kommen morgen
zurück; *to get something back*
etwas zurückbekommen
get in **hereinkommen**; (arrive)
ankommen
get off (bus, etc.) **aussteigen**
get on (bus, etc.) **einsteigen**
get out **herauskommen**;
(bring out) **herausholen**
get up (rise) **aufstehen**
gift **das Geschenk**
gin **der Gin**
ginger (spice) **der Ingwer**
girl **das Mädchen**
girlfriend **die Freundin**
give **geben**
glad **froh**
glass **das Glas**
glasses **die Brille**
gloves **die Handschuhe**
glue **der Leim, der Klebstoff**
go **gehen**; (travel) **fahren**;
(by plane) **fliegen**
gold **das Gold**
good **gut**
goodbye **Auf Wiedersehen**
good night **Guten Abend**
government **die Regierung**
granddaughter **die Enkelin**
grandfather **der Großvater**
grandmother **die Großmutter**
grandparents **die**
Großeltern (m pl)
grandson **der Enkel**
grapes **die Trauben** (f pl)
grass **das Gras**
Great Britain **Großbritannien**
great: great! **prima!**
green **grün**
grey **grau**
grill **der Grill**
grilled **gegrillt**
grocer's **das**
Lebensmittelgeschäft
ground floor **das Erdgeschoss**
groundsheet **der Zeltboden,**

die Bodenplane
guarantee **die Garantie**;
(verb) **garantieren**
guard **der Wächter**
guest **der Gast**
guide **der Führer**
guide book **der (Reise)führer**
guided tour **die Führung**
guitar **die Gitarre**
gun (rifle) **das Gewehr**;
(pistol) **die Pistole**
gutter **die Dachrinne**

H

hair **das Haar**
haircut **der Haarschnitt**
hairdresser's **der Friseur**; (ladies')
der Friseursalon
hair dryer **der Fön**
hair spray **das Haarspray**
half **halb**; *half an hour*
eine halbe Stunde
half board **Halbpension**
half-brother **der Halbbruder**
half-sister **die Halbschwester**
ham **der gekochte Schinken**
hamburger **der Hamburger**
hammer **der Hammer**
hamster **der Hamster**
hand **die Hand**
handbag **die Handtasche**
handbrake **die Handbremse**
handle (door) **die Klinke**
hand luggage **das Handgepäck**
handshake **der Händedruck**
handsome **gut aussehend**
hangover **der Kater**
happy **glücklich**
harbour **der Hafen**
hard **hart**; (difficult) **schwer**
hardware shop **der**
Eisenwarenhändler
hat **der Hut**
have (verb) **haben**: *I have*
ich habe; *you have*
(singular informal) **du hast**;
(plural informal) **ihr habt**;
(singular formal; plural formal)
Sie haben; *we have* **wir**
haben; *they have* **sie haben**;
do you have ...? **haben Sie ...?**;
I have to go **ich muss gehen**
hay fever **der Heuschnupfen**
he **er**
head **der Kopf**
headache **die Kopfschmerzen**;
headache pill **die**
Kopfschmerztablette
headlights **die Scheinwerfer**
head office **die Zentrale**

headphones **der Kopfhörer**
hear **hören**
hearing aid **das Hörgerät**
heart **das Herz**
heart condition: I have a heart
condition **Ich bin herzkrank**
hearts (cards) **Herz**
heater **das Heizgerät**
heating **die Heizung**
heavy **schwer**
hedge **die Hecke**
heel (shoe) **der Absatz**;
(foot) **die Ferse**
hello **guten Tag**;
(on phone) **hallo**
help **die Hilfe**; (verb) **helfen**
her: it's her **sie ist es**;
it's for her **es ist für sie**;
give it to her **geben sie es ihr**;
her book **ihr Buch**;
her shoes **ihre Schuhe**;
it's hers **es gehört ihr**
hi **hallo**
high **hoch**
hiking **das Wandern**
hill **der Berg**
him: it's him **er ist es**; *it's for him*
es ist für ihn; *give it to him*
geben sie es ihm
hire **leihen, mieten**
his: his book **sein Buch**;
his shoes **seine Schuhe**;
it's his **es gehört ihm**
history **die Geschichte**
hitchhike **trampen**
HIV positive **HIV positiv**
hobby **das Hobby**
holiday **die Ferien,**
der Urlaub
Holland **Holland**
home: at home **zu Hause**
homeopathy **die Homöopathie**
honest **ehrlich**
honey **der Honig**
honeymoon **die Hochzeitsreise**
horn (car) **die Hupe**;
(animal) **das Horn**
horrible **schrecklich**
hospital **das**
Krankenhaus
host **der/die Gastgeber(in)**
hour **die Stunde**
house **das Haus**
household products **die**
Haushaltswaren (f pl)
how? **wie?**
humanities **die**
Geisteswissenschaften (f pl)
hundred **hundert**
hungry: I'm hungry
ich habe Hunger

hurry: I'm in a hurry
   ich bin in Eile
husband der (Ehe)mann

I

I ich
ice das Eis
ice cream die Eiscreme
ice lolly das Eis am Stiel
ice skates die Schlittschuhe
ice-skating: to go ice-skating
   Schlittschuh laufen
   gehen
if wenn
ignition die Zündung
ill krank
immediately sofort
impossible unmöglich
in in; in English auf
   Englisch; in the hotel
   im Hotel
indicator der Blinker
indigestion die
   Magenverstimmung
infection die Infektion,
   die Entzündung
information die Information
injection die Spritze
injury die Verletzung
ink die Tinte
inn das Gasthaus
inner tube der Schlauch
insect das Insekt
insect repellent das
   Insektenmittel
insomnia die Schlaflosigkeit
instant coffee der Pulverkaffee
insurance die Versicherung
interesting interessant
internet das Internet
interpret dolmetschen
interpreter der/die
   Dolmetscher(in)
intravenous drip die
   intravenöse Infusion
invitation die Einladung
invoice die Rechnung
Ireland Irland
Irish irisch
Irishman der Ire
Irishwoman die Irin
iron (material) das Eisen;
   (for clothes) das Bügeleisen;
   (verb) bügeln
is: he/she/it is... er/sie/es ist...
island die Insel
it es
Italian der/die Italiener(in);
   (adj) italienisch
Italy Italien

J

jacket die Jacke
jam die Marmelade,
   die Konfitüre
January Januar
jazz der Jazz
jeans die Jeans
jellyfish die Qualle
jeweller's das Juweliergeschäft
jewellery der Schmuck
job die Arbeit
jog (verb) joggen; to go for
   a jog joggen gehen
joke der Witz
journey die Fahrt, die Reise
July Juli
jumper der Pullover
June Juni
just (only) nur; it's just arrived
   es ist gerade angekommen

K

kettle der Wasserkessel
key der Schlüssel
keyboard die Tastatur
kidney die Niere
kilo das Kilo
kilometre der Kilometer
kitchen die Küche
knee das Knie
knife das Messer
knit stricken
knitwear die Strickwaren (f pl)
know wissen; (be acquainted
   with) kennen; I don't know
   ich weiß nicht

L

label das Etikett
lace die Spitze
laces (shoe) die Schnürsenkel
   (m pl)
lady die Dame
lake der See
lamb (animal) das Lamm; (meat)
   das Lammfleisch
lamp die Lampe
lampshade der Lampenschirm
land das Land; (verb) landen
language die Sprache
laptop der Laptop
large groß
last (final) letzter;
   last week letzte Woche;
   at last! endlich!
late spät; the bus is late
   der Bus hat Verspätung
later später

laugh lachen
launderette der Waschsalon
laundry (place) die Wäscherei;
   (dirty clothes) die Wäsche
lawn der Rasen
lawnmower der Rasenmäher
lawyer der Rechtsanwalt/
   die Rechtsanwältin
laxative das Abführmittel
lazy faul
lead die Leine
lead-free bleifrei
leaf das Blatt
leaflet die Broschüre,
   der Flyer
learn lernen
leather das Leder
lecture theatre der
   Vorlesungssaal
leeks das Breitlauch,
   der Porrée
left (not right) links;
   there's nothing left
   es ist nichts mehr übrig
left luggage locker das
   Gepäckschließfach
left side die linke Seite
leg das Bein
lemon die Zitrone
lemonade die Limonade
length die Länge
lens die Linse
less weniger
lesson die Stunde
letter (post) der Brief; (alphabet)
   der Buchstabe
letter box der Briefkasten
lettuce der Kopfsalat
library die Bibliothek,
   die Bücherei
licence die Genehmigung;
   (driving) der Führerschein
life das Leben
lift (in building) der Fahrstuhl;
   could you give me a lift? können
   Sie mich mitnehmen?
light das Licht; (adj) leicht;
   (not dark) hell
light bulb die (Glüh)birne
lighter das Feuerzeug; lighter fuel
   das Feuerzeugbenzin
light meter der
   Belichtungsmesser
like: I like you ich mag Sie;
   I like swimming ich
   schwimme gern; it's like...
   es ist wie...; like this so
lime (fruit) die Limette
lip salve der Lippen-Fettstift
lipstick der Lippenstift
liqueur der Likör

list die Liste
litre der Liter
litter der Abfall
litter bin die Mülleimer
little (small) klein; it's a little big
es ist ein bisschen zu groß;
just a little nur ein bisschen
liver die Leber
lobster der Hummer
lollipop der Lutscher
long lang
lorry der Lastwagen
lost property das Fundbüro
lot: a lot viel
loud laut; (colour) grell
lounge das Wohnzimmer;
(in hotel) die Lounge
love die Liebe; (verb) lieben
low niedrig; (voice) tief
luck das Glück; good luck!
viel Glück!
luggage der Koffer, das
Gepäck; luggage rack
die Gepäckablage
lunch das Mittagessen
Luxembourg Luxemburg

M

mad verrückt
magazine die Zeitschrift
maid das Zimmermädchen
mail die Post
main courses die Hauptgerichte
main road die Hauptstraße
make machen
make-up das Make-up
man der Mann
manager der Geschäftsführer
many: not many nicht viele
map (of country)
die Landkarte;
(of town) der Stadtplan
marble der Marmor
March März
margarine die Margarine
market der Markt
marmalade die
Orangenmarmelade
married verheiratet
mascara das Maskara,
die Wimperntusche
mass (church) die Messe
match (light) das Streichholz;
(sport) das Spiel
material (fabric) der Stoff
matter: it doesn't matter
das macht nichts
mattress die Matratze
maybe vielleicht
me: it's me ich bin's;

it's for me es ist für mich;
give it to me geben Sie es mir
meal das Essen
mean: what does this mean?
was bedeutet das?
meat das Fleisch
mechanic der/die
Mechaniker(in)
medication die Medikamente
medicine die Medizin
meeting die Besprechung,
das Treffen
melon die Melone
men's toilets die Herrentoilette
menu die Speisekarte
message die Nachricht
metro station die U-Bahnstation
microwave die Mikrowelle
midday der Mittag
middle: in the middle
in der Mitte
midnight Mitternacht
milk die Milch
mine: it's mine es gehört mir
mineral water das mineralwasser
minute die Minute
mirror der Spiegel
Miss Fräulein
mistake der Fehler
mobile phone das Handy,
das Mobiltelefon
modem das Modem
modern architecture die moderne
Architektur
Monday Montag
money das Geld
monitor der Monitor,
der Bildschirm
month der Monat
monument das Denkmal
moon der Mond
moped das Moped
more mehr
morning der Morgen; in the
morning am Morgen
mother die Mutter
motorbike das Motorrad
motorboat das Motorboot
motorway die Autobahn
mountain der Berg
mountain bike
das Mountain-Bike
mouse die Maus
mousse (for hair)
der Schaumfestiger
moustache der Schnurrbart
mouth der Mund
move (verb) bewegen;
(house) umziehen;
don't move! stillhalten!
movie der Film

Mr Herr
Mrs Frau
Ms Frau
much viel
mum die Mama
Munich München
museum das Museum
mushroom der Pilz
music die Musik
musical instrument das
Musikinstrument
musician der/die Musiker(in)
music system die Musikanlange
mussels die Muscheln (f pl)
must: I must... ich muss...
mustard der Senf
my: my book mein Buch;
my keys meine Schlüssel

N

nail (metal, finger) der Nagel
nail clippers der Nagelzwicker
nailfile die Nagelfeile
nail polish der Nagellack
name der Name; what's your
name? wie heißen Sie?
napkin die Serviette
nappy die Windel
narrow eng
near nah; near the door nahe der
Tür; near London in der Nähe
von London
necessary notwendig
neck der Hals
necklace die Halskette
need (verb) brauchen; I need...
ich brauche...; there's no need
das ist nicht nötig
needle die Nadel
negative (photo) das Negativ
nephew der Neffe
Netherlands die Niederlande
never nie
new neu
news die Nachrichten
newsagent's der Zeitungsladen
newspaper die Zeitung
New Zealand Neuseeland
New Zealander der/die
Neuseeländer(in)
next nächster;
next week nächste Woche
nice (attractive) hübsch;
(pleasant) angenehm;
(to eat) lecker
niece die Nichte
night die Nacht
nightclub der Nachtklub
nightdress das Nachthemd
night porter der Nachtportier

nine **neun**

nineteen **neunzehn**

ninety **neunzig**

no (response) **nein;**
  I have no money
  ich habe kein Geld

noisy **laut**

north **der Norden**

Northern Ireland **Nordirland**

North Sea **die Nordsee**

nose **die Nase**

not **nicht**

notebook **das Notizbuch**

notepad **der Notizblock**

notes **die Banknoten** (f pl)

nothing **nichts**

novel **der Roman**

November **November**

now **jetzt**

nowhere **nirgendwo**

number **die Zahl;**
  (telephone) **die Nummer**

number plate **das**
  Nummernschild

nurse (man) **der**
  Krankenpfleger; (woman)
  die Krankenschwester

nut (fruit) **die Nuss;**
  (for bolt) **die Mutter**

O

occasionally **gelegentlich**

October **Oktober**

of **von;** the name of the hotel
  der Name des Hotels

office **das Büro**

often **oft**

oil **das Öl**

ointment **die Salbe**

OK **okay**

old **alt;** how old are you?
  wie alt sind Sie?

olive **die Olive**

omelette **das Omelette**

on... **auf...**

one (number) **eins;**
  one beer/sausage
  ein Bier/eine Wurst

one million **eine Million**

onion **die Zwiebel**

only **nur**

open (verb) **öffnen;**
  (adj) **offen**

opening times
  die Öffnungszeiten

opera **die Oper**

operating theatre
  der Operationssaal

operation **die Operation**

operator **die Vermittlung**

opposite: opposite the hotel
  gegenüber dem Hotel

optician **Augenarzt/**
  Augenärztin

or **oder**

orange (colour) **orange;**
  (fruit) **die Orange**

orange juice **der Orangensaft**

orchestra **das Orchester**

ordinary **gewöhnlich**

other: the other...
  der/die/das andere...

our **unser;** it's ours **es gehört uns**

out **aus;** he's out
  er ist nicht da

outside **außerhalb**

oven **der Backofen**

over (more than) **über;** (finished)
  vorbei; (across) **über;**
  over there **dort drüben**

overtake **überholen**

oyster **die Auster**

P

package (parcel) **das Paket**

packet **das Paket;**
  (cigarettes) **die Schachtel**

pack of cards **das Kartenspiel**

padlock **das Vorhängeschloss**

page **die Seite**

pain **der Schmerz**

painkiller (medicine)
  die Schmerztablette

paint **die Farbe**

pair **das Paar**

palace **der Palast**

pale **blass**

pancake **der Pfannkuchen**

paper **das Papier;** (newspaper)
  die Zeitung

paraffin **das Paraffin**

parcel **das Paket**

pardon? **wie bitte?**

parents **die Eltern** (m pl)

park **der Park;** (verb) **parken;**
  no parking **Parken verboten**

parsley **die Petersilie**

parting (hair) **der Scheitel**

party (celebration) **die Party;**
  (group) **die Gruppe;**
  (political) **die Partei**

passenger **der Fahrgast,**
  der Passagier

passport **der Pass, der Ausweis;**
  passport control
  die Passkontrolle

password **das Passwort**

pasta **die Nudeln**

pastry **das Gebäck**

path **der Weg**

pavement **der Bürgersteig**

pay **bezahlen**

payment **die Bezahlung**

peach **der Pfirsich**

peanuts **die Erdnüsse** (f pl)

pear **die Birne**

pearl **die Perle**

peas **die Erbsen** (f pl)

pedestrian **der Fußgänger**

pedestrian zone
  die Fußgängerzone

peg (clothes) **die**
  Wäscheklammer;
  (tent) **der Hering**

pen **der Stift**

pencil **der Bleistift;**
  pencil sharpener **der**
  Bleistiftspitzer

penfriend **der/die**
  Brieffreund(in)

penicillin **das Penizillin**

penknife **das**
  Taschenmesser

people **die Leute** (m pl)

pepper **der Pfeffer;** (red/green)
  der Paprika

peppermints **die**
  Pfefferminzbonbons

per: per night **pro Nacht**

perfect **perfekt**

perfume **das Parfüm**

perhaps **vielleicht**

perm **die Dauerwelle**

pet passport **der Tierpass**

petrol **das Benzin**

petrol station **die Tankstelle**

pets **die Haustiere** (nt pl)

pharmacy **die Apotheke**

phonecard **die Telefonkarte**

photocopier **der Fotokopierer**

photograph **das Foto;**
  (verb) **fotografieren**

photographer **der Fotograf**

phrase book **der Sprachführer**

piano **das Klavier**

pickpocket **der Taschendieb**

picnic **das Picknick**

piece **das Stück**

pill **die Tablette**

pillow **das Kopfkissen**

pilot **der/die Pilot(in)**

pin **die Stecknadel**

PIN (number) **die Geheimzahl**

pineapple **die Ananas**

pink **rosa**

pipe (for smoking) **die Pfeife;** (for
  water) **die Pumpe, das Rohr**

piston **der Kolben**

place **der Platz;** (town, etc.) **der**
  Ort; at your place **bei Ihnen**

plant **die Pflanze**

plaster (for cut) das Pflaster
plastic das Plastik
plastic bag die Tragetasche,
   die Plastiktüte
plate der Teller
platform das Gleis,
   der Bahnsteig
play (theatre) das Stück;
   (verb) spielen
please bitte
plug (electrical) der Stecker;
   (sink) der Stöpsel
plumber der/die Klempner(in)
pocket die Tasche
poison das Gift
Poland Polen
Pole (man) der Pole;
   (woman) die Polin
police die Polizei
police officer der/die Polizist(in)
police report der Polizeibericht
police station das Polizeirevier
Polish polnisch
politics die Politik
poor arm; (bad quality) schlecht
pop music die Popmusik
pork das Schweinefleisch
port (harbour) der Hafen
porter (hotel) der Portier
possible möglich
post die Post; (verb) aufgeben
postbox der Briefkasten
postcard die Postkarte
postcode die Postleitzahl
poster das Poster
postman/woman
   der/die Briefträger(in)
post office das Postamt
potato die Kartoffel
pottery die Töpferei
poultry das Geflügel
pound (money, weight)
   das Pfund
pram der Kinderwagen
prawns die Krabben (f pl)
prefer: I prefer... ich
   mag lieber...
pregnant schwager
prescription das Rezept
presentation der Vortrag
pretty (beautiful) schön;
   (quite) ziemlich;
   pretty good recht gut
price der Preis
priest Geistliche
printer der Drucker
private privat
problem das Problem
professor der/die Professor(in)
profits der Gewinn
public öffentlich

public holiday der Feiertag
pull ziehen
puncture die Reifenpanne
purple lila
purse das Portemonnaie
push drücken
pushchair der Sportwagen
put legen, stellen, setzen
pyjamas der Schlafanzug

Q

quality die Qualität
quarter das Viertel
quay der Kai
question die Frage
queue die Schlange;
   (verb) anstehen
quick schnell
quiet still, ruhig
quite (fairly) ziemlich; (fully) ganz

R

rabbit das Kaninchen
radiator der Heizkörper;
   (car) der Kühler
radio das Radio
radish der Rettich; (small red)
   das Radieschen
railway die Bahn
rain der Regen
raincoat der Regenmantel
raisins die Rosinen (f pl)
rake der Rechen
rare (uncommon) selten;
   (steak) blutig
raspberries die Himbeeren (f pl)
rat die Ratte
razor blades die Rasierklingen
   (f pl)
read lesen
reading lamp die Leselampe
ready fertig
ready meals die Fertiggerichte
   (nt pl)
rear lights die Rücklichter (f pl)
receipt die Quittung
reception der Empfang
receptionist die
   Empfangsperson
record (music) die Schallplatte;
   (sporting, etc.) der Rekord
record shop das
   Schallplattengeschäft
red rot
refreshments die
   Erfrischungen (f pl)
registered post das Einschreiben
relative der Verwandte
relax sich entspannen

religion die Religion
remember sich erinnern;
   I don't remember
   ich erinnere mich nicht
rent (verb) mieten
report der Bericht
research die Forschungen
reservation die
   Reservierung
rest (remainder) der Rest;
   (verb) sich ausruhen
restaurant das Restaurant
return (come back)
   zurückkommen;
   (give back) zurückgeben
return ticket die Rückfahrkarte
rhubarb der Rhabarber
rice der Reis
rich reich
right (correct) richtig;
   (direction) rechts
right side die rechte Seite
ring (jewellery) der Ring;
   (verb: to call) anrufen
ripe reif
river der Fluss
road die Straße
roasted geröstet
robbery der Diebstahl
rock (stone) der Stein;
   (music) der Rock
roll (bread) das Brötchen
roof das Dach
room das Zimmer;
   (space) der Raum
room service der Zimmerservice
rope das Seil
rose die Rose
round (circular) rund
rubber (eraser) der
   Radiergummi;
   (material) der Gummi
rubbish der Abfall
ruby (stone) der Rubin
rucksack der Rucksack
rug (mat) der Läufer;
   (blanket) die Wolldecke
ruins die Ruinen (f pl)
ruler (for drawing) das Lineal
rum der Rum
run (verb) laufen
runway die Start-und
   Landebahn

S

sad traurig
safe sicher
safety pin die Sicherheitsnadel
sailing das Segeln
sailing boat das Segelboot

salad der Salat
salami die Salami
sale (at lower prices)
der Schlussverkauf
sales der Absatz
salmon der Lachs
salt das Salz
same: the same dress das gleiche
Kleid; *same again please*
nochmal dasselbe, bitte
sand der Sand
sandals die Sandalen (f pl)
sandwich das Sandwich,
das Butterbrot
sanitary towels die
Damenbinden (f pl)
Saturday Samstag
sauce die Soße
saucepan der Kochtopf
saucer die Untertasse
sauna die Sauna
sausage die Wurst
say sagen; *what did you say?* was
haben Sie gesagt?; *how do
you say...?* wie sagt man...?
Scandinavia Skandinawien
scarf der Schal; (head)
das Kopftuch
schedule der Zeitplan
school die Schule
scissors die Schere
Scotland Schottland
Scotsman der Schotte
Scotswoman die Schottin
Scottish schottisch
screen der Bildschirm
screw die Schraube
screwdriver der
Schraubenzieher
sea das Meer
seafood die
Meeresfrüchte (f pl)
seat der Sitz
seat belt der Sicherheitsgurt
second (time) die Sekunde;
(in series) zweiter;
second class zweiter Klasse
secretary der/die Sekretär(in)
see sehen; *I can't see* ich kann
nichts sehen; *I see* ich
verstehe; *see you soon*
bis bald; *see you tomorrow*
bis Morgen
self-employed selbständig
sell verkaufen
seminar das Seminar
separate getrennt
separated: we are separated
wir leben getrennt
separately getrennt
September September

serious ernst
serviette die Serviette
seven sieben
seventeen siebzehn
seventy siebzig
several mehrere
sew nähen
shampoo das Shampoo
shave: to have a shave
sich rasieren
shaving foam die Rasiercreme
shawl das Umhängetuch
she sie
sheet das (Bett)laken
shell die Muschel
shellfish (as food) die
Meeresfrüchte (f pl)
sherry der Sherry
ship das Schiff
shirt das Hemd
shoelaces die Schnürsenkel
(m pl)
shoe polish die Schuhcreme
shoe shop das Schuhgeschäft
shoes die Schuhe (m pl)
shop das Geschäft
shopkeeper der/die
Verkäufer(in)
shopping das Einkaufen;
(items bought) die
Einkäufe; *to go shopping*
einkaufen gehen
short kurz
shorts die Shorts
shoulder die Schulter
shower (bath) die Dusche;
(rain) der Schauer
shower gel das Duschgel
shutter (camera)
der Verschluss; (window)
der Fensterladen
sick (ill) krank; *I feel sick* mir ist
übel; *to be sick* (vomit)
sich übergeben
side die Seite; (edge)
die Kante
sidelights das Standlicht
sightseeing die Besichtigungen
sign das Schild
silk die Seide
silver (metal) das Silber;
(colour) silber
simple einfach
sing singen
singing das Singen
single (one) einziger; (unmarried)
ledig, single
single room das Einzelzimmer
single ticket die einfache
Fahrkarte
sister die Schwester

sister-in-law die Schwägerin
six sechs
sixteen sechzehn
sixty sechzig
ski (verb) Ski fahren
ski binding die Skibindung
ski boots die Skistiefel (m pl)
skid (verb) schleudern
skiing: to go skiing
Skifahren gehen
ski lift der Skilift
skin cleanser der Hautreiniger
ski resort der Skiurlaubsort
skirt der Rock
skis die Skier (m pl)
ski sticks die Skistöcke
(m pl)
sky der Himmel
sledge der Schlitten
sleep der Schlaf;
(verb) schlafen
sleeping bag der Schlafsack
sleeping pill die Schlaftablette
sleeve der Ärmel
slice of... das Stück...
slippers die Pantoffeln (m pl)
slow langsam
small klein
smell der Geruch;
(verb) riechen
smile das Lächeln;
(verb) lächeln
smoke der Rauch;
(verb) rauchen
snack der Imbiss
snow der Schnee
so so; *not so much* nicht so viel
soaking solution
(for contact lenses) die
Aufbewahrungslösung
soap die Seife
socks die Socken (f pl)
soda water das Sodawasser
sofa die Couch, das Sofa
soft weich
soil die Erde
somebody jemand
somehow irgendwie
something etwas
sometimes manchmal
somewhere irgendwo
son der Sohn
song das Lied
sorry! (apology) Verzeihung!,
Entschuldigung!; *I'm sorry*
es tut mir Leid; *sorry?*
(pardon) wie bitte?
soup die Suppe
south der Süden
South Africa Südafrika
souvenir das Souvenir

spa **der Kurort**

spade (shovel) **der Spaten**

spades (cards) **Pik**

spanner **der Schraubenschlüssel**

spares **die Ersatzteile** (nt pl)

spark(ing) plug **die Zündkerze**

speak **sprechen**; *do you speak English?* **sprechen Sie Englisch?**; *I don't speak German* **ich spreche kein Deutsch**

speed **die Geschwindigkeit**

spider **die Spinne**

spinach **der Spinat**

spoon **der Löffel**

sport **der Sport**; *sports centre* **das Sportzentrum**

spring (mechanical) **die Feder**; (season) **der Frühling**

square (shape) **das Quadrat**; (in town) **der Platz**

stadium **das Stadion**

staircase **die Treppe**

stairs **die Treppe**

stamp **die Briefmarke**

stand **der Stand**

stapler **der Hefter**

star **der Stern**; (film) **der Star**

start **der Start, der Anfang**; (verb) **anfangen**

starters **die Vorspeisen** (f pl)

statement **die Aussage**

station **der Bahnhof**; (underground) **die Station**

statue **die Statue**

steak **das Steak**

steal **stehlen**; *it's been stolen* **es ist gestohlen worden**

steamed **gedämpft**

steamer (boat) **der Dampfer**; (cooking) **der Dampfkochtopf**

steering wheel **das Lenkrad**

stepdaughter **der Stieftochter**

stepfather **der Stiefvater**

stepmother **der Stiefmutter**

stepson **der Stiefsohn**

still water **Wasser ohne Kohlensäure, das Tafelwasser**

sting **der Stich**; (verb) **stechen**

stockings **die Strümpfe** (m pl)

stomach **der Magen**

stomachache **die Magenschmerzen**

stop (bus stop) **die Haltestelle**; (verb) **anhalten**; *stop!* **halt!**

storm **der Sturm**

strawberries **die Erdbeeren** (f pl)

stream (**water**) **der Bach**

street **die Straße**

string (cord) **der Faden**; (guitar, etc.) **die Saite**

strong (person, drink) **stark**; (material) **stabil**; (taste) **streng**

student **der/die Student(in)**

stupid **dumm**

suburbs **der Stadtrand**

sugar **der Zucker**

suit **der Anzug**; *it suits you* **es steht Ihnen**

suitcase **der Koffer**

sun **die Sonne**

sunbathe **sonnenbaden**

sunburn **der Sonnenbrand**

Sunday **Sonntag**

sunglasses **die Sonnenbrille**

sunny: it's sunny **es ist sonnig**

sunshade **der Sonnenschirm**

suntan: to get a suntan **braun werden**

suntan lotion **das Sonnenöl**

suntanned **braungebrannt**

superior **Vorgesetzte**

supermarket **der Supermarkt**

supper **das Abendessen**

supplement **der Zuschlag**

suppository **das Zäpfchen**

sure **sicher**

surname **der Nachname**

sweat **der Schweiß**; (verb) **schwitzen**

sweatshirt **das Sweatshirt**

sweet (not sour) **süß**; (confectionery) **die Süßigkeit, der Bonbon**

swim (verb) **schwimmen**

swimming **das Schwimmen**

swimming costume **der Badeanzug**

swimming pool **das Schwimmbad**

swimming trunks **die Badehose**

Swiss **der/die Schweizer(in)**; (adj) **schweizerisch**

switch **der Schalter**

Switzerland **die Schweiz**

swivel chair **der Drehstuhl**

synagogue **die Synagoge**

syringe **die Spritze**

syrup **der Sirup**

T

table **der Tisch**

tablet **die Tablette**

take **nehmen**

take-away **der Schnellimbiss**

take-off **der Abflug**

talcum powder **der Puder**

talk **das Gespräch**; (verb) **reden**

tall **groß**

tampons **die Tampons** (m pl)

tangerine **die Mandarine**

tap **der Hahn**

tapestry **der Wandteppich**

taxi **das Taxi**

taxi rank **der Taxistand**

tea **der Tee**; *black tea* **der schwarze Tee**; *tea with milk* **der Tee mit Milch**

teacher **der/die Lehrer(in)**

tea towel **das Geschirrtuch**

telephone **das Telefon**; (verb) **telefonieren**

telephone box **die Telefonzelle**

television **das Fernsehen**; *to watch television* **fernsehen**

temperature **die Temperatur**; (fever) **das Fieber**

ten **zehn**

tennis **das Tennis**

tent **das Zelt**

ten thousand **zehntausend**

tent peg **der Hering**

tent pole **die Zeltstange**

terminal **das Terminal**

terrace **die Terrasse**

than: bigger than **größer als**

thank (verb) **danken**; *thanks* **danke**; *thank you* **danke schön**

that: that man **dieser Mann**; *that woman* **diese Frau**; *what's that?* **was ist das?**; *I think that...* **ich denke, dass...**

the **der** (masculine singular); **die** (feminine singular); **das** (neuter singular); **die** (plural)

theatre **das Theater**

their: their room **ihr Zimmer**; *their books* **ihre Bücher**; *it's theirs* **es gehört ihnen**

them: it's them **sie sind es**; *it's for them* **es ist für sie**; *give it to them* **geben Sie es ihnen**

then **dann**

there **da**; *there is/are...* **es gibt...**; *is/are there...?* **gibt es...?**

these **diese**

they **sie**

thick **dick**

thief **der Dieb**

thin **dünn**

think **denken**;

I think so ich glaube ja;
I'll think about it ich überlege
es mir
third dritter
thirsty durstig; *I'm thirsty*
ich habe Durst
thirteen dreizehn
thirty Dreißig
this: this man dieser Mann; *this woman* diese Frau; *what's this?* was ist das?; *this is Mr...*
das ist Herr...
those diese da; *those things*
die Dinge dort
thousand tausend
three drei
three hundred dreihundert
throat die Kehle
throat pastilles die
Halstabletten (f pl)
through durch
thunderstorm das Gewitter
Thursday Donnerstag
ticket die Karte; *ticket kiosk*
der Schalter
tide: high tide die Flut;
low tide die Ebbe
tie die Krawatte;
(verb) festmachen
tight eng
tights die Strumpfhose
tiles die Kacheln (f pl)
time die Zeit; *what's the time?*
wie spät ist es?
timetable (train, bus)
der Fahrplan
tin die Dose
tin opener der Dosenöffner
tip (money) das Trinkgeld;
(end) die Spitze
tired müde
tissues die Taschentücher
to: to England nach England;
to the station zum Bahnhof;
to the doctor zum Arzt
toast der Toast
tobacco der Tabak
toboggan der Schlitten
today heute
together zusammen
toilet die Toilette
toilet paper das Toilettenpapier
tomato die Tomate
tomato juice der Tomatensaft
tomorrow morgen
tongue die Zunge
tonic das Tonic
tonight heute abend
too (also) auch; (excessively) zu
tooth der Zahn
toothache die Zahnschmerzen

toothbrush die Zahnbürste
toothpaste die Zahnpasta
torch die Taschenlampe
tour die Rundreise
tour guide der/die
Reiseleiter(in)
tourist der/die Tourist(in)
tourist office das
Verkehrsbüro, das
Fremdenverkehrsbüro
towel das Handtuch
tower der Turm
town die Stadt
town hall das Rathaus
toy das Spielzeug
track suit der Trainingsanzug
tractor der Traktor
trade fair die Handelsmesse
tradition die Tradition
traffic der Verkehr
traffic jam der Stau
traffic lights die Ampel
trailer der Anhänger
train der Zug
trainee der/die Auszubildende
trainers die Turnschuhe
tram die Straßenbahn
translate übersetzen
translator der/die Übersetzer(in)
travel agency das Reisebüro
tray das Tablett
tree der Baum
trolley der Kofferkuli
trousers die Hose
true wahr
try versuchen
Tuesday Dienstag
tunnel der Tunnel
Turk (man) der Türke;
(woman) die Türkin
Turkey die Türkei
Turkish türkisch
tweezers die Pinzette
twelve zwölf
twenty zwanzig
twin beds die zwei
Einzelbetten
two zwei
typewriter die Schreibmaschine
tyre der Reifen

U

ugly hässlich
umbrella der (Regen)schirm
uncle der Onkel
under... unter...
underground die U-Bahn
underpants die Unterhose
underskirt der Unterrock
understand verstehen;

I don't understand
ich verstehe nicht
underwear die Unterwäsche
university die Universität
unleaded bleifrei
until bis
unusual ungewöhnlich
up oben; *up there* da oben
upwards nach oben
urgent dringend
us: it's us wir sind es; *it's for us*
es ist für uns; *give it to us*
geben sie es uns
use der Gebrauch;
(verb) gebrauchen; *it's no use*
es hat keinen Zweck
useful hilfreich
usual gewöhnlich
usually gewöhnlich

V

vacancy (room) ein
freies Zimmer
vaccination die Impfung
vacuum cleaner der
Staubsauger
valley das Tal
valuables die Wertsachen (f pl)
valve das Ventil
vanilla die Vanille
vase die Vase
veal das Kalbfleisch
vegetable das Gemüse
vegetarian der/die
Vegetarier(in);
(adj) vegetarisch
vehicle das Fahrzeug
very sehr
vest das (Unter)hemd
vet der Tierarzt
video (tape, film) das Video;
video recorder
der Videorecorder;
video tape die Videocassette
Vienna Wien
view der Blick
viewfinder der Sucher
villa die Villa
village das Dorf
vinegar der Essig
violin die Geige
visit der Besuch;
(verb) besuchen
visiting hours die Besuchszeit
visitor der/die Besucher(in)
vitamin tablet die
Vitamintablette
vodka der Wodka
voice die Stimme
voicemail die Voice-mail

W

wait **warten**;
  wait! **warten Sie!**
waiter **der Ober**;
  waiter! **Herr Ober!**
waiting room **das Wartezimmer**; (station) **der Wartesaal**
waitress **die Kellnerin**;
  waitress! **Fräulein!**
Wales **Wales**
walk **der Spaziergang**;
  (verb) **gehen**; to go for a walk **spazieren gehen**
wall (inside) **die Wand**;
  (outside) **die Mauer**
wallet **die Brieftasche**
war **der Krieg**
wardrobe **der Kleiderschrank**
warm **warm**
was: I was **ich war**;
  he/she/it was **er/sie/es war**
wash basin **das Waschbecken**
washing powder **das Waschpulver**
washing-up liquid **das Spülmittel**
wasp **die Wespe**
watch **die (Armband)uhr**;
  (verb) **ansehen**
water **das Wasser**
waterfall **der Wasserfall**
water heater **das Heißwassergerät**
wave **die Welle**;
  (verb: with hand) **winken**
wavy (hair) **wellig**
we **wir**
weather **das Wetter**
web site **die Webseite**
wedding **die Hochzeit**
Wednesday **Mittwoch**
weeds **das Unkraut**
week **die Woche**
welcome **willkommen**;
  you're welcome **keine Ursache**
well-done (steak) **durchgebraten**
wellingtons **die Gummistiefel**
Welsh **walisisch**
Welshman/woman **der/die Waliser(in)**
were: you were (singular informal) **du warst**; (singular formal; plural) **Sie waren**; we/they were **wir/sie waren**
west **der Westen**
wet **naß**
what? **was?**
wheel **das Rad**

wheelchair **der Rollstuhl**;
  wheelchair access **der Rollstuhlfahrer**
when? **wann?**
where? **wo?**
whether **ob**
which? **welcher?**
whisky **der Whisky**
white **weiß**
who? **wer?**
why? **warum?**
wide **breit**
wife **die (Ehe)frau**
wind **der Wind**
window **das Fenster**;
  window box **der Blumenkasten**
windscreen **die Windschutzscheibe**
wine **der Wein**
wine list **die Weinkarte**
wing **der Flügel**
with **mit**
without **ohne**
witness **der/die Zeuge(in)**
woman **die Frau**
women's toilets **die Damentoilette**
wood (material) **das Holz**
wool **die Wolle**
word **das Wort**
work **die Arbeit**; (verb) **arbeiten**; (machine, etc.) **funktionieren**
worktop **die Arbeitsfläche**
worse **schlechter**
worst **schlechtester**
wrapping paper **das Packpapier**; (for presents) **das Geschenkpapier**
wrist **das Handgelenk**
writing paper **das Schreibpapier**
wrong **falsch**

X, Y, Z

x-ray **die Röntgenaufnahme**
x-ray department **die Röntgenabteilung**
year **das Jahr**
yellow **gelb**
yes **ja**
yesterday **gestern**
yet: is it ready yet? **ist es schon fertig?**; not yet **noch nicht**
yoghurt **der Jogurt**
you (singular informal) **du**;
  (singular formal; plural) **Sie**;
  for you **für dich/Sie**;
  with you **mit dir/Ihnen**

your (singular informal) **dein**;
  (singular formal; plural) **Ihr**;
  your shoes **deine/Ihre Schuhe**
yours: is this yours?
  (singular informal) **gehört das dir?** (singular formal; plural) **gehört das Ihnen?**
youth hostel **die Jugendherberge**
zip **der Reißverschluß**
zoo **der Zoo**

DICTIONARY
German to English

The gender of German nouns listed here is indicated by the abbreviations *m* for masculine, *f* for feminine, and *nt* for neuter. Plural nouns are followed by the abbreviations *m pl*, *f pl*, and *nt pl*. The feminine form of most occupations and personal attributes is made by adding **-in** to the masculine form: **Buchhalter(in)** *accountant*, for example. Exceptions to this rule are listed separately. Where necessary, adjectives are denoted by the abbreviation *adj*.

A

Abend (m) *evening*
Abendessen (nt)
  dinner, supper
aber *but*
Abfahrt (f) *departure*
Abfall (m) *litter, rubbish*
Abfertigungsschalter (m)
  check-in (desk)
Abflug (m) *departures,*
  take-off; **Abflughalle** (f)
  departure lounge
Abführmittel (nt)
  laxative
Absatz (m) *heel (shoe);*
  sales (figures)
absichtlich *deliberately*
Abteil (nt) *compartment*
Abteilung (f) *department*
acht *eight*
achtzehn *eighteen*
achtzig *eighty*
Adapter (m) *adaptor*
Adresse (f) *address*
Aids *Aids*
Aktentasche (f) *briefcase*
Alkohol (m) *alcohol*
alle(s) *all, every;* **alle Straßen** *all*
  the streets; **das ist alles** *that's*
  all; **alles** *everything*
allein *alone*
allergisch *allergic*
alt *old;* **wie alt sind Sie?**
  how old are you?
am *at, next to;* **am Bahnhof**
  at the station; **am Fenster**
  next to the window
Amerika *America*
Amerikaner(in) (m/f)
  American (person)
amerikanisch *American (adj)*
Ampel (f) *traffic lights*
Ananas (f) *pineapple*
andere *another (different);* **der/**
  die/das andere... *the other...;*
  ein anderes Zimmer
  another room; **das ist etwas**
  anderes! *that's different!;*
  etwas anderes *something else;*
  jemand anders *someone else;*
  woanders *somewhere else;*
  ein andermal *another time*
Anfang (m) *start*
anfangen *to start*
Anfänger (m) *beginner*
Angeln (nt) *fishing;*
  Angeln gehen *to go fishing*
angenehm *nice, pleasant*
anhalten *to stop*
Anhänger (m) *trailer*
ankommen *to arrive*
Ankunft (f) *arrivals*
Anrufbeantworter (m)
  answering machine
anrufen *to ring, call*
ansehen *to watch*
anstehen *to queue*
Antiquitätengeschäft (nt)
  antique shop
Antiseptikum (nt) *antiseptic*
Antragsformular (nt)
  application form
Anzug (m) *suit*
Aperitif (m) *aperitif*
Apfel (m) *apple*
Apotheke (f) *pharmacy*
Appetit (m) *appetite*
Aprikose (f) *apricot*
Arbeit (f) *job, work*
arbeiten *to work*
Arbeitsfläche (f) *worktop*
arm *poor (not rich)*
Arm (m) *arm*
Armband (nt) *bracelet*
Armbanduhr (f) *watch*
Ärmel (m) *sleeve*
Arzt (m) *doctor*
Aschenbecher (m) *ashtray*
Asthma (nt) *asthma*
atmen *to breathe*
attraktiv *attractive*
auch *too (also)*
auf... *on/at/in...;* **auf der Post**
  at the post office; **auf Englisch**
  in English

Aufbewahrungslösung (f)
  soaking solution (for
  contact lenses)
aufgeben *to post*
aufstehen *to get up (rise)*
Auf Wiedersehen *goodbye*
Auge (nt) *eye;* **die Augen** *eyes*
Augenarzt/Augenärztin (m/f)
  optician
Augenbraue (nt) *eyebrow*
August *August*
aus *out*
Ausflug (m) *excursion*
Ausgang (m) *exit*
ausgezeichnet *excellent*
Ausländer(in) *foreigner*
Auspuff (m) *exhaust*
ausruhen: sich ausruhen
  to rest
Aussage (f) *statement*
außerhalb *outside*
aussteigen *to get off (bus, etc.)*
Ausstellung (f) *exhibition*
Auster (f) *oyster*
Australien *Australia*
Australier(in) (m/f)
  Australian (person)
australisch *Australian (adj)*
Ausweis (m) *passport*
Auszubildende (m/f) *trainee*
Auto (nt) *car*
Autobahn (f) *motorway*
automatisch *automatic*

B

Baby (nt) *baby*
Bach (m) *stream*
backen *to bake*
Bäcker (m) *baker*
Bäckerei (f) *bakery*
Backofen (m) *oven*
Bad (nt) *bath;* **ein Bad nehmen**
  to have a bath
Badeanzug (m)
  swimming costume
Badehose (f)
  swimming trunks

Badewanne (f) *bathtub*
Badezimmer (nt) *bathroom*
Bahn (f) *railway*
Bahnhof (m) *station*
Bahnsteig (m) *platform*
Balkon (m) *balcony*
Ball (m) *ball*
Ballett (nt) *ballet*
Banane (f) *banana*
Band (f) *band* (musicians)
Bank (f) *bank*
Banknoten (f pl) *(bank)notes*
Bar (f) *bar* (drinks)
Bargeld (nt) *cash*; **bar bezahlen**
to pay cash
Bart (m) *beard*
Batterie (f) *battery*
Bauarbeiter(in) *builder*
Bauer (m) *farmer*
Bauernhof (m) *farm*
Baum (m) *tree*
Baumwolle (f) *cotton*
Bayern *Bavaria*
Becken (nt) *basin* (sink)
bedeutet: was bedeutet das?
what does this mean?
behindert *disabled*
beide *both*; **wir beide**
both of us
beige *beige*
bei Ihnen *at your place*
Bein (nt) *leg*; **Beinbruch** (m)
broken leg
Beispiel (nt) *example*; **zum**
Beispiel *for example*
beißen *to bite*
Belag (m) *filling* (in sandwich)
Belgien *Belgium*
Belgier(in) (m/f)
Belgian (person)
belgisch *Belgian* (adj)
Belichtungsmesser (m)
light meter
Benzin (nt) *petrol*
Berater(in) *consultant*
Berg (m) *hill, mountain*
Bericht (m) *report*
Berliner (m) *doughnut*
beschäftigt *busy* (occupied)
Bescheinigung (f) *certificate*
besetzt *engaged* (occupied)
Besichtigungen (f) *sightseeing*
besonders *especially*
Besprechung (f) *meeting*
besser *better*
Basteln (nt) *DIY*
bester *best*
bestreiten *to deny*
Besuch (m) *visit*
besuchen *to visit*
Besucher(in) (m/f) *visitor*

Besuchszeit (f) *visiting hours*
betrunken *drunk*
Bett (nt) *bed*
Bettlaken (nt) *sheet*
Bettwäsche (f) *bed linen*
bewegen *to move*
bezahlen *to pay*
Bezahlung (f) *payment*
BH (m) *bra*
Bibliothek (f) *library*
Bier (nt) *beer*
Bikini (m) *bikini*
Bildschirm (m) *screen, monitor*
billig *cheap*
bin: ich bin *I am*
Biochemie (f) *biochemistry*
Birne (f) *pear*
bis *until*; **bis Freitag**
by Friday; **bis Morgen**
see you tomorrow;
bis bald *see you soon*
Biss (m) *bite* (by dog, etc.)
bißchen *a little*; **es ist**
ein bisschen zu groß
it's a little big; **nur ein**
bisschen *just a little*
bist: du bist *you are* (informal)
bitte *please*; **wie bitte?** *pardon?*
bitter *bitter*
Blase (f) *blister*
blass *faint* (unclear), *pale*
Blatt (nt) *leaf*
blau *blue*
blaue Fleck (m) *bruise*
bleichen *to bleach* (hair)
Bleichmittel (nt) *bleach*
bleifrei *unleaded*
Bleistift (m) *pencil*
Bleistiftspitzer (m)
pencil sharpener
Blick (m) *view*
blind *blind* (cannot see)
Blinker (m) *indicator*
Blitz (m) *flash* (camera)
blond *blond* (adj)
Blume (f) *flower*
Blumenbeet (nt) *flowerbed*
Blumenkasten (m)
window box
Blumenkohl (m) *cauliflower*
Blumenladen (m) *florist*
Blumenstecken (nt)
flower-arranging
Bluse (f) *blouse*
Blut (nt) *blood*
blutig *rare* (steak)
Blutprobe (f) *blood test*
Boden (m) *bottom, floor, ground*;
Bodenplane (f) *groundsheet*
Bohnen (f pl) *beans*
Boiler (m) *boiler*

Bonbon (m) *sweet* (candy)
Boot (nt) *boat* (small)
Bordkarte (f) *boarding pass*
Botschaft (f) *embassy*
Boxen (nt) *boxing*
braten *fry*
Bratpfanne (f) *frying pan*
brauchen *to need*; **ich**
brauche... I need...
braun *brown*; **braun werden**
to get a suntan
braungebrannt *suntanned*
breit *wide*
Breitlauch (nt) *leeks*
Bremse (f) *brake*
bremsen *to brake*
brennen *to burn*
Bridge (nt) *bridge* (game)
Brief (m) *letter* (post)
Brieffreund(in) (m/f)
penfriend
Briefkasten (m) *letter box,
postbox*
Briefmarke (f) *stamp*
Brieftasche (f) *wallet*
Briefträger(in) (m/f)
postman(woman)
Briefumschlag (m) *envelope*
Brille (f) *glasses*
britisch *British*
Brombeere (f) *blackberry*
Brosche (f) *brooch*
Broschüre (f) *brochure, leaflet*
Brot (nt) *bread*
Brötchen (nt) *bread roll*
Brücke (f) *bridge*
Bruder (m) *brother*
Brunnen (m) *fountain*
Brüssel *Brussels*
Brust (f) *chest* (part of body)
Buch (nt) *book*
buchen *to book*
Bücherei (f) *library*
Buchhalter(in) (m/f)
accountant
Buchhandlung (f) *bookshop*
Buchstabe (m) *letter* (alphabet)
Budget (nt) *budget*
Bügeleisen (nt) *iron* (for clothes)
bügeln *to iron*
Burg (f) *castle*
Bürgersteig (m) *pavement*
Büro (nt) *office*
Bürste (f) *brush*
bürsten *to brush* (hair)
Bus (m) *bus*
Busbahnhof (m)
bus/coach station
Büstenhalter (m) *bra*
Butter (f) *butter*
Butterbrot (nt) *sandwich*

C

Café (nt) *café*
Campinggas (nt) *camping gas*
Campingplatz (m) *campsite*
Campingplatzverwaltung (f)
  campsite office
Chips (f) *crisps*
Compact-Disc (f)
  compact disc
Computer (m) *computer*
Computerspiele (nt pl)
  computer games
Couch (f) *sofa*
Creme (f) *cream (lotion)*
Curry (nt) *curry*

D

da *there*
Dach (nt) *roof*
Dachboden (m) *attic*
Dachrinne (f) *gutter*
Dame (f) *lady, woman*
Damenbinden (f pl)
  sanitary towels
Damentoilette (f)
  women's toilets
Dampfer (m) *steamer (boat)*
Dampfkochtopf (m)
  steamer (cooking)
Däne *Dane (man)*
Dänemark *Denmark*
Dänin *Dane (woman)*
dänisch *Danish*
danken *to thank;*
  danke *thanks;*
  danke schön *thank you*
dann *then*
das (nt) *the;*
  das ist Herr... *this is Mr...*
Dauerwelle (f) *perm*
Decke (f) *blanket; ceiling*
dein(e) *your (sing, informal)*
Delegierte(r) *delegate*
denken *to think*
Denkmal (nt) *monument*
Deodorant (nt) *deodorant*
der *the (masculine)*
deutsch *German (adj);* **Deutsch**
  German (language)
Deutsche (m/f) *German (person)*
Deutschland *Germany*
Dezember *December*
Diabetiker(in) *diabetic*
Diamant (m) *diamond (gem)*
dick *fat (adj: person); thick*
die *the (feminine and plural)*
Dieb (m) *thief*
Diebstahl (m) *robbery*
Dienstag *Tuesday*

diese: diese Frau
  that/this woman
Diesel (m) *diesel*
dieser: dieser Mann
  that/this man
Dirigent (m) *conductor
  (orchestra)*
Dokument (nt) *document*
Dollar (m) *dollar*
dolmetschen *to interpret*
Dolmetscher(in) (m/f)
  interpreter
Dom (m) *cathedral*
Donau: die Donau *Danube*
Donnerstag *Thursday*
Doppelzimmer (nt)
  double room
Dorf (nt) *village*
dort drüben *over there*
Dose (f) *can, tin;* **Dosenöffner**
  (m) *tin opener*
Drahtseilbahn (f) *cable car*
Drehstuhl (m) *swivel chair*
drei *three*
dreihundert *three hundred*
Dreißig *thirty*
dreizehn *thirteen*
dringend *urgent*
dritter *third*
drücken *to push*
Drucker (m) *printer*
du *you (singular informal)*
dumm *stupid*
dunkel *dark*
dünn *thin*
durch *through*
Durchfall (m) *diarrhoea*
durchgebraten *well-done (meat)*
Durst (m) *thirst;* **ich habe Durst**
  I'm thirsty
durstig *thirsty*
Dusche (f) *shower*
Duschgel (nt) *shower gel*

E

Ebbe (f) *low tide*
Ecke (f) *corner*
Ehefrau (f) *wife*
Ehemann (m) *husband*
ehrlich *honest*
Ei (nt) *egg*
Eile: ich bin in Eile
  I'm in a hurry
Eimer (m) *bucket*
Einbrecher (m) *burglar*
einchecken *to check in*
einer von beiden *either
  of them*
einfach *simple;* **einfache
  Fahrkarte** (f) *single ticket*

Einfahrt (f) *driveway*
Eingang (m) *entrance*
Einkäufe (f) *shopping
  (items bought)*
Einkaufen (nt) *shopping (activity);*
  einkaufen gehen
  to go shopping
Einladung (f) *invitation*
einlösen *to cash*
eins *one (number);*
  ein Bier/eine Wurst
  one beer/one sausage
Einschreiben (nt)
  registered post
einsteigen *to get on (bus, etc.)*
Eintrittskarte (f)
  entrance ticket
Eintrittspreis (m)
  admission charge
Einwegwindeln (f pl)
  disposable nappies
Einzelzimmer (nt) *single room*
einziger *single (one)*
Eis (nt) *ice, ice cream;*
  Eiscreme (f) *ice cream;*
  Eis am Stiel (nt) *ice lolly*
Eisen (nt) *iron (metal)*
Eisenwarenhändler (m)
  hardware shop
elastisch *elastic*
Elektriker(in) (m/f) *electrician*
elektrisch *electric*
elf *eleven*
Ellbogen (m) *elbow*
Eltern (m pl) *parents*
Empfang (m) *reception*
Empfangsperson (m/f)
  receptionist
Ende (nt) *end*
endlich! *at last!*
eng *narrow, tight*
England *England*
Engländer(in) (m/f)
  Englishman(woman)
englisch *English (adj);* **Englisch**
  English (language)
Enkel (m) *grandson*
Enkelin (f) *granddaughter*
Entschuldigung! *excuse me!,
  sorry!*
entweder... oder...
  either... or...
entwickeln *to develop (film)*
Entzündung (f) *infection*
Epilektiker(in) (m/f) *epileptic*
er *he*
Erbsen (f pl) *peas*
Erdbeeren (f pl) *strawberries*
Erde (f) *soil*
Erdgeschoss (nt) *ground floor*
Erdnüsse (f pl) *peanuts*

Erfrischungen (f pl) *refreshments*
erinnern: sich erinnern
 to remember; **ich erinnere**
 mich nicht *I don't remember*
Erkältung (f) *cold (illness);* **ich**
 bin erkältet *I have a cold*
Ermäßigungen (f) *discounts*
ernst *serious*
Ersatzteile (nt pl) *spares*
Erste Hilfe (f) *first aid*
erster *first;* **erster Klasse** *first*
 class; **erste Stock** (m) *first floor*
es *it*
Essen (nt) *food, meal;*
 essen *to eat*
Essig (m) *vinegar*
Etikett (nt) *label*
etwa: etwa 16 *about 16*
etwas *something*

F

Faden (m) *string (cord)*
Fahne (f) *flag*
Fähre (f) *ferry*
fahren *to drive, go (travel)*
Fahrer(in) (m/f) *driver*
Fahrgast (m) *passenger*
Fahrplan (m) *timetable*
 (train, bus)
Fahrpreis (m) *fare*
Fahrrad (nt) *bicycle*
Fahrstuhl (m) *lift (in building)*
Fahrt (f) *journey*
Fahrzeug (nt) *vehicle*
fair *fair (just)*
falsch *wrong*
Familie (f) *family*
Fan (m) *fan (enthusiast)*
fantastisch *fantastic*
Farbe (f) *colour, paint*
Farbfilm (m) *colour film*
fast *almost*
faul *lazy*
Februar *February*
Feder (f) *spring (mechanical)*
Fehler (m) *mistake*
Feiertag (m) *public holiday*
Feige (f) *fig*
Feinkostgeschäft (nt)
 delicatessen
Feld (nt) *field*
Fenster (nt) *window*
Fensterladen (m) *shutter*
Ferien (f) *holiday*
Fernsehen (nt) *television;*
 fernsehen *to watch television*
Ferse (f) *heel (foot)*
fertig *ready;* **Fertiggerichte**
 (nt pl) *ready meals*
festmachen *to tie*

Fett (nt) *fat*
feucht *damp*
Feuer (nt) *fire*
Feuerlöscher (m)
 fire extinguisher
Feuerwerk (nt) *fireworks*
Feuerzeug (nt) *lighter*
Feuerzeugbenzin (nt)
 lighter fuel
Fieber (nt) *temperature,*
 fever
Film (m) *film, movie*
Filter (m) *filter*
Filterpapier (nt) *filter papers*
Finger (m) *finger*
Fisch (m) *fish*
Fischgeschäft (nt) *fishmonger's*
flach *flat (level)*
Flasche (f) *bottle*
Flaschenöffner (m)
 bottle opener
Fleisch (nt) *meat*
Fliege (f) *fly (insect)*
fliegen *to fly*
Floh (m) *flea*
Flohspray (nt) *flea spray*
Flöte (f) *flute*
Flug (m) *flight*
Flügel (m) *wing*
Flughafen (m) *airport*
Flughafenbus (m) *airport bus*
Fluglinie (f) *airline*
Flugnummer (f)
 flight number
Flugsteig (m) *gate*
 (at airport)
Flugzeug (nt) *aircraft*
Fluss (m) *river*
Flut (f) *high tide*
Flyer (m) *leaflet, flyer*
Fön (m) *hair dryer*
Forschungen (f) *research*
Foto (nt) *photograph*
Fotograf (m) *photographer*
fotografieren *to photograph*
Fotokopierer (m) *photocopier*
Frage (f) *question*
Frankreich (nt) *France*
Franzose (m) *Frenchman*
Französin (f) *Frenchwoman*
französisch *French*
Frau *Mrs*
Frau *Ms*
Frau (f) *woman, wife*
Fräulein *Miss;*
 Fräulein! *waitress!*
frei *free*
Freitag *Friday*
Fremdenverkehrsbüro (nt)
 tourist office
Freund(in) (m/f) *friend*

freundlich *friendly*
freut mich *pleased to meet you*
Friedhof (m) *cemetery*
Friseur (m) *hairdresser's*
Friseursalon (m)
 ladies' hairdresser's
Fritten (m pl) *chips*
froh *glad*
Frost (m) *frost;*
Frucht (f) *fruit;* **Fruchtsaft** (m)
 fruit juice
früh *early*
Frühling (m) *spring (season)*
Frühstück (nt) *breakfast*
fühlen *to feel (touch)*
Führer (m) *guide*
Führerschein (m)
 driving licence
Führung (f) *guided tour*
Füllung (f) *filling (in tooth, cake)*
Fundbüro (nt) *lost property*
fünf *five*
fünfzehn *fifteen*
fünfzig *fifty*
funktionieren *to work*
 (machine, etc.)
für *for;* **für mich** *for me;*
 wofür? *what for?;*
 für eine Woche
 for a week
furchtbar *awful*
Fuß (m) *foot;* **Füße** (m pl) *feet*
Fußball (m) *football*
Fußboden (m) *floor (ground)*
Fußgänger (m) *pedestrian;*
 Fußgängerzone (f)
 pedestrian zone

G

Gabel (f) *fork*
Gang (m) *aisle*
ganz *quite (fully)*
Garage (f) *garage (for parking)*
Garantie (f) *guarantee*
garantieren *to guarantee*
Garten (m) *garden*
Gartenarbeit (f) *gardening*
Gartencenter (nt)
 garden centre
Gärtner(in) (m/f) *gardener*
Gaspedal (nt) *accelerator*
Gast (m) *guest*
Gastgeber(in) (m/f) *host*
Gasthaus (nt) *inn*
Gebäck (nt) *pastry*
Gebäude (nt) *building*
geben *to give*
Gebiet (nt) *field of work*
Gebiss (m) *dentures,*
 false teeth

geboren to be born:
  ich bin in... geboren
  I was born in...
gebraten fried
Gebrauch (m) use
gebrauchen to use
gebrochen broken (arm, etc.)
Geburtstag (m) birthday;
  Herzlichen Glückwunsch!
  happy birthday!
Geburtstagsgeschenk (nt)
  birthday present
Geburtstagskarte (f)
  birthday card
gedämpft steamed
gefährlich dangerous
Geflügel (nt) poultry
Gefrierschrank (m) freezer
gegen against
gegenüber opposite
gegrillt grilled
Geheimzahl (f) PIN (number)
gehen to go, walk;
  gehen Sie weg! go away!
Geige (f) violin
Geisteswissenschaften
  (f pl) humanities
Geistliche (m/f) priest
gekocht boiled
gekochte Schinken (m) ham
Gel (nt) gel (hair)
gelb yellow
Geld (nt) money
Geldautomat (m)
  cash machine (ATM)
Geldschein (m) banknote
gelegentlich occasionally
Gemüse (nt) vegetable
Genehmigung (f) licence
genug enough
Gepäck (nt) luggage
Gepäckablage (f) luggage rack
Gepäckausgabe (f)
  baggage claim
Gepäckschließfach (nt)
  left luggage locker
gerade just; **es ist gerade**
  angekommen it's just arrived
gerecht fair (just)
gern: ich schwimme gern
  I like swimming
geröstet roasted
Geruch (m) smell
Geschäft (nt) business, shop
Geschäftsführer
  (m) manager
Geschenk (nt) gift;
  Geschenkpapier (nt)
  wrapping paper
Geschichte (f) history
geschieden divorced

Geschirrspülmaschine (f)
  dishwasher
Geschirrtuch (nt)
  tea towel
geschlossen closed
Geschmack (m) flavour
Geschwindigkeit (f) speed
Gesicht (nt) face
Gespräch (nt) talk
gestern yesterday
Getränk (nt) drink
getrennt separate(ly);
  wir leben getrennt
  we are separated
Getriebe (nt) gearbox
Gewehr (nt) gun (rifle)
Gewinn (m) profits
Gewitter (nt) thunderstorm
gewöhnlich ordinary,
  usual, usually
gibt: es gibt... there is/are...;
  gibt es...? is/are there...?
Gift (nt) poison
Gin (m) gin
Gitarre (f) guitar
Glas (nt) glass
glaube: ich glaube ja
  I think so
gleiche: the same; **gleiche**
  Kleid the same dress
Gleis (nt) platform
Glocke (f) bell (church)
Glück (nt) luck; **viel Glück!**
  good luck!
glücklich happy
Glühbirne (f) light bulb
Gold (nt) gold
Grafiker(in) (m/f) designer
Gras (nt) grass
gratis free (no charge)
grau grey
grell loud (colour)
Grenze (f) border
Grill (m) barbecue, grill
groß big, large, tall;
  größer als bigger than
Großbritannien Great Britain
Großeltern (m pl) grandparents
Großmutter (f) grandmother
Großstadt (f) city
Großvater (m) grandfather
grün green
Grund (m) bottom (sea)
Gruppe (f) party (group)
Gummi (m) rubber (material)
Gummiband (nt) elastic band
Gummistiefel (nt) wellingtons
Gurke (f) cucumber
Gürtel (m) belt
gut good; **mir ist nicht gut**
  I don't feel well

gut aussehend handsome
Guten Abend good night
guten Tag hello, good day

H

Haar (nt) hair
Haarschnitt (m) haircut
Haarspray (nt) hair spray
Haarspülung (f) conditioner
haben have; **ich habe...** I have...;
  haben Sie...? do you have...?
Hafen (m) harbour, port
Hahn (m) tap
Hähnchen (nt) chicken (cooked)
halb half; **eine halbe Stunde**
  half an hour
Halbbruder (m) half-brother
Halbpension half board
Halbschwester (f) half-sister
hallo hello (on phone); hi
Hals (m) neck
Halsband (nt) collar
Halskette (f) necklace
Halstabletten (f pl)
  throat pastilles
halt! stop!
Haltestelle (f) stop (bus stop)
Hamburger (m) hamburger
Hammer (m) hammer
Hamster (m) hamster
Hand (f) hand
Handbremse (f) handbrake
Händedruck (m) handshake
Handelsmesse (f) trade fair
Handgelenk (nt) wrist
Handgepäck (nt) hand luggage
Handschuhe (f) gloves
Handtasche (f) handbag
Handtuch (nt) towel
Handy (nt) mobile phone
hart hard
hässlich ugly
Hauptgericht (nt) main course
Hauptstraße (f) main road
Haus (nt) house;
  zu Hause at home
Haushaltswaren (f pl)
  household products
Hausmeister(in) caretaker
Haustiere (nt pl) pets
Hautreiniger (m) skin cleanser
Hecke (f) hedge
Hefter (m) stapler
Heftzwecke (f) drawing pin
heiß hot; **mir ist heiß**
  I feel hot
heißen to be called;
  wie heißt das? what's it
  called?; **wie heißen Sie?**
  what's your name?

Heißwassergerät (nt)
  water heater
Heizgerät (nt) *heater*
Heizkörper (m) *radiator*
Heizung (f) *heating*
helfen *to help*
hell *light* (not dark)
Hemd (nt) *shirt*
herauskommen *to get out*
Herd (m) *cooker*
hereinkommen *to come in*
Hering (m) *tent peg*
Herr *Mr*
Herrenfriseur (m) *barber's*
Herrentoilette (f)
  men's toilets
herunter *down*
Herz (nt) *heart, hearts* (cards);
  ich bin herzkrank *I have*
  a heart condition
herzlichen Glückwunsch!
  congratulations!
Heuschnupfen (m) *hay fever*
heute *today*; **heute**
  abend *tonight*
Hilfe (f) *help*
hilfreich *useful*
Himbeeren (f pl) *raspberries*
Himmel (m) *sky*
hinter... *behind*...
HIV positiv *HIV positive*
Hobby (nt) *hobby*
hoch *high*
Hochzeit (f) *wedding*
Hochzeitsreise (f) *honeymoon*
Höhle (f) *cave*
holen *to get* (fetch)
Holland *Holland*
Holländer(in) (m/f)
  Dutchman(woman)
holländisch *Dutch* (adj)
Holz (nt) *wood* (material)
Homöopathie (f)
  homeopathy
Honig (m) *honey*
hören *hear*
Hörgerät (nt) *hearing aid*
Horn (nt) *horn* (animal)
Hose (f) *trousers*
Hosenträger (nt pl) *braces*
hübsch *nice* (attractive)
Huhn (nt) *chicken* (animal)
Hummer (m) *lobster*
Hund (m) *dog*
hundert *hundred*
Hunger (m) *hunger*; **ich habe**
  Hunger *I'm hungry*
Hupe (f) *horn* (car)
husten *to cough*;
  Husten (m) *cough*
Hut (m) *hat*

I

ich *I*; **ich bin** *I am*
ihr(e) *their/her*; *your*
  (singular formal)
im: im Hotel *in the*
  hotel
Imbiss (m) *snack*
immer *always*
Impfung (f) *vaccination*
in *in*; **in der Nacht** *at night*
Infektion (f) *infection*
Information (f) *information*
Ingwer (m) *ginger* (spice)
Insekt (nt) *insect*
Insektenmittel (nt)
  insect repellent
Insel (f) *island*
interessant *interesting*
Internet (nt) *internet*
intravenöse Infusion (f)
  intravenous drip
Ire (m) *Irishman*
irgendwie *somehow*
irgendwo *somewhere*
Irin (f) *Irishwoman*
irisch *Irish*
Irland *Ireland*
ist *is*; **er/sie/es ist**...
  he/she/it is...
Italien *Italy*
Italiener(in) (m/f) *Italian*
italienisch *Italian* (adj)

J

ja *yes*
Jacke (f) *jacket*
Jahr (nt) *year*
Jahrmarkt (m) *fair,*
  funfair
Jalousie (f) *blinds*
Januar *January*
Jazz (m) *jazz*
Jeans (f) *jeans*
jeder *each, every,*
  everyone
jemand *somebody*
jetzt *now*
joggen *to jog*;
  joggen gehen
  to go for a jog
Jogurt (m) *yoghurt*
Jucken (nt) *itch*
Jugendherberge (f)
  youth hostel
Juli *July*
Junge (m) *boy*
Juni *June*
Juweliergeschäft (nt)
  jeweller's

K

Kabelfernsehen (nt)
  cable TV
Kacheln (f pl) *tiles*
Kaffee (m) *coffee*;
  Kaffee ohne Milch
  black coffee
Käfig (m) *cage*
Kai (m) *quay*
Kalbfleisch (nt) *veal*
kalt *cold* (adj);
  mir ist kalt *I am cold*
Kamera (f) *camera*
Kamm (m) *comb*
Kanada *Canada*
Kanadier(in) (m/f)
  Canadian (person)
kanadisch *Canadian* (adj)
Kanal (m) *canal* (m)
  English Channel
Kanaltunnel (m)
  Channel Tunnel
Kaninchen (nt) *rabbit*
kann ich... haben?
  can I have...?
Kante (f) *side* (edge)
Kanu (nt) *canoe*
kaputt *broken* (machine, etc.)
Karo *diamonds* (cards)
Karotte (f) *carrot*
Karte (f) *card, ticket*;
  Kartenspiel (nt)
  pack of cards
Kartoffel (f) *potato*
Käse (m) *cheese*
Kasse (f) *box office, checkout*
Kassette (f) *cassette*
Kassettenrecorder (m)
  cassette player
Kassierer(in) (m/f) *cashier*
Kater (m) *hangover*
Katze (f) *cat*
kaufen *to buy*
Kaufhaus (nt)
  department store
Kaugummi (m) *chewing gum*
Kaution (f) *deposit*
Kehle (f) *throat*
kehren *to sweep*
Keilriemen (m) *fan belt*
kein *not any*;
  ich habe kein Geld
  I don't have any money
keine Ursache *you're welcome*
Keller (m) *cellar*
Kellnerin (f) *waitress*
kennen *to know* (to be
  acquainted with)
Kerze (f) *candle*
Kilo (nt) *kilo*

Kilometer (m) *kilometre*
Kind (nt) *child*
Kinder *children*
Kinderbett (nt) *cot*
Kindersitz (m) *car seat*
Kinderstation (f)
  children's ward
Kinderwagen (m) *pram*
Kino (nt) *cinema*
Kirche (f) *church*
Kirmes (f) *fair, funfair*
Kirsche (f) *cherry*
Kissen (nt) *cushion*
klar *clear*
Klasse (f) *class*
klassische Musik (f)
  classical music
Klavier (nt) *piano*
Kleid (nt) *dress*
Kleider (nt pl) *clothes*
Kleiderbügel (m) *coat hanger*
Kleiderschrank (m) *wardrobe*
klein *little, small*
Kleingeld (nt) *change (money)*
kleinschneiden *to chop, cut*
Klempner(in) (m/f) *plumber*
Klimaanlage (f) *air conditioning*
Klingel (f) *(door) bell*
Klinke (f) *handle (door)*
Klub (m) *club*
klug *clever*
Knie (nt) *knee*
Knoblauch (m) *garlic*
Knöchel (m) *ankle*
Knochen (m) *bone*
Knopf (m) *button*
Koch (m) *cook*
kochen *to boil, cook*
Kochtopf (m) *saucepan*
Köder (m) *bait*
Koffer (m) *suitcase;*
  Kofferkuli (m) *luggage trolley*
Kofferraum (m) *boot (car)*
Kohl (m) *cabbage*
Kolben (m) *piston*
Köln *Cologne*
komisch *funny*
kommen *to come;* **ich komme
  aus...** *I come from...;* **kommen
  Sie her!** *come here!*
Kommode (f) *chest of drawers*
kompliziert *complicated*
Konditorei (f) *cake shop*
Kondom (nt) *condom*
Konferenz (f) *conference*
Konferenzzimmer (nt)
  conference room
Konfitüre (f) *jam*
können Sie...? *can you...?*
Konsulat (nt) *consulate*
Kontaktlinsen (f) *contact lenses*

Konzert (nt) *concert*
Kopf (m) *head*
Kopfhörer (m) *headphones*
Kopfkissen (nt) *pillow*
Kopfsalat (m) *lettuce*
Kopfschmerzen (m) *headache*
Kopftuch (nt) *headscarf*
Korb (m) *basket*
Korken (m) *cork*
Korkenzieher (m) *corkscrew*
Körper (m) *body*
Korridor (m) *corridor*
Kosmetika (f) *cosmetics*
kosten *to cost;* **was kostet das?**
  what does it cost?
kostenlos *free (no charge)*
Kostenvoranschlag (m) *estimate*
Kotelett (nt) *chop (food)*
Krabbe (f) *crab*
Krabben (f pl) *prawns*
Kragen (m) *collar*
Krampf (m) *cramp*
krank *ill, sick*
Krankenhaus (nt) *hospital*
Krankenpfleger (m) *nurse (man)*
Krankenschwester (f)
  nurse (woman)
Krankenwagen (m) *ambulance*
Krawatte (f) *tie*
Krebs (m) *crayfish*
Kreditkarte (f) *credit card*
Kreuz *clubs (cards)*
Kreuzfahrt (f) *cruise*
Krieg (m) *war*
Krücken (f pl) *crutches*
Küche (f) *kitchen*
Kuchen (m) *cake*
kühl *cool*
Kühler (m) *radiator (car)*
Kühlschrank (m) *fridge*
Kunde (m) *client*
Kunst (f) *art*
Kunstgalerie (f) *art gallery*
Künstler(in) (m/f) *artist*
Kupplung (f) *clutch*
Kurort (m) *spa*
kurz *short*
Kusine (f) *cousin (female)*

L

Lächeln (nt) *smile;*
  lächeln *to smile*
lachen *to laugh*
Lachs (m) *salmon*
Ladegerät (nt) *charger*
Lagerfeuer (nt) *campfire*
Lamm (nt) *lamb (animal)*
Lammfleisch (nt) *lamb (meat)*
Lampe (f) *lamp*
Lampenschirm (m) *lampshade*

Land (nt) *country, land*
landen *to land*
Landkarte (f) *map (of country)*
lang *long*
Länge (f) *length*
langsam *slow*
langweilig *boring*
Laptop (m) *laptop (computer)*
Lastwagen (m) *lorry*
laufen *to run*
Läufer (m) *rug (mat)*
laut *loud, noisy*
Leben (nt) *life*
Lebensmittelgeschäft (nt)
  grocer's
Lebensmittelvergiftung (f)
  food poisoning
Leber (f) *liver*
lecker *nice (to eat)*
Leder (nt) *leather*
ledig *single (unmarried)*
leer *empty*
Leerung (f) *collection (postal)*
legen *to put*
Lehrer(in) *teacher*
Leiche (f) *body (corpse)*
leicht *easy, light (not heavy)*
Leid: es tut mir Leid *I'm sorry*
leihen *to hire*
Leim (m) *glue*
Leine (f) *lead*
Lenkrad (nt) *steering wheel*
lernen *to learn*
Leselampe (f) *reading lamp*
lesen *to read*
letzter *last (final);*
  letzte Woche *last week*
Leute (m pl) *people*
Licht (nt) *light*
lieb *dear (person)*
Liebe (f) *love*
lieben *to love;* **ich mag lieber...**
  I prefer...
Lied (nt) *song*
Lieferung (f) *delivery*
Liegestuhl (m) *deck chair*
Likör (m) *liqueur*
lila *purple*
Limette (f) *lime (fruit)*
Limonade (f) *lemonade*
Lineal (nt) *ruler*
  (for drawing)
links *left (not right);*
  linke Seite (f) *left side*
Linse (f) *lens*
Lippen-Fettstift (m) *lip salve*
Lippenstift (m) *lipstick*
Liste (f) *list*
Liter (m) *litre*
Locken (f pl) *curls*
Löffel (m) *spoon*

Lounge (f) *lounge* (in hotel)
Luft (f) *air*
Luftmatratze (f) *air mattress*
Luftpost (f) *airmail*
Lutscher (m) *lollipop*
Luxemburg *Luxembourg*

M

machen *to make;* **macht nichts**
   it doesn't matter
Mädchen (nt) *girl*
Magen (m) *stomach;*
   Magenschmerzen (f)
   stomachache;
   Magenverstimmung (f)
   indigestion
Mail (f) *e-mail;* **Mail Adresse** (f)
   e-mail address
Make-up (nt) *make-up*
Maler(in) *decorator*
Manager(in) *executive*
manchmal *sometimes*
Mandarine (f) *tangerine*
Mann (m) *man, husband*
Manschettenknöpfe (m pl)
   cufflinks
Mantel (m) *coat*
Margarine (f) *margarine*
Markt (m) *market*
Marmelade (f) *jam*
Marmor (m) *marble*
März *March*
Maskara (nt) *mascara*
Matratze (f) *mattress*
Mauer (f) *wall* (outside)
Maus (f) *mouse*
Mechaniker(in) *mechanic*
Medikamente (f) *medication*
Medizin (f) *medicine*
Meer (nt) *sea;* **Meeresfrüchte**
   (f pl) *seafood, shellfish*
Mehl (nt) *flour*
mehr *more;* **Mehrgepäck** (nt)
   excess baggage
mehrere *several*
mein(e) *my*
Melone (f) *melon*
Messe (f) *mass* (church)
Messer (nt) *knife*
Metzgerei (f) *butcher's*
mieten *to rent*
Mikrowelle (f) *microwave*
Milch (f) *milk*
Million *million*
   eine Million *one million*
Mineralwasser (nt)
   mineral water
Minute (f) *minute*
mir: es gehört mir *it's mine*
mit *with*

Mittag (m) *midday;*
   Mittagessen (nt) *lunch*
Mitte (f) *centre, middle;*
   in der Mitte *in the middle*
Mitternacht *midnight*
Mittwoch *Wednesday*
Möbel (f) *furniture*
Mobiltelefon (nt) *mobile phone*
möchten Sie...?
   would you like...?
Mode (f) *fashion*
Modem (nt) *modem*
moderne Architektur (f)
   modern architecture
möglich *possible;*
   so bald wie möglich
   as soon as possible
Möhre (f) *carrot*
Molkereiprodukte
   (nt pl) *dairy products*
Monat (m) *month*
Mond (m) *moon*
Monitor (m) *monitor*
Montag *Monday*
Moped (nt) *moped*
Morgen (m) *morning;* **am**
   Morgen *in the morning;*
   morgen *tomorrow*
Motor (m) *engine* (motor)
Motorboot (nt) *motorboat*
Motorhaube (f) *bonnet* (car)
Motorrad (nt) *motorbike*
Mountain-Bike (nt)
   mountain bike
müde *tired*
Mülleimer (f) *litter bin*
Müllsack (m) *bin liner*
Mülltonne (f) *dustbin*
München *Munich*
Mund (m) *mouth*
Münze (f) *coin*
Muschel (f) *shell*
Muscheln (f pl) *mussels*
Museum (nt) *museum*
Musik (f) *music;*
   Musikanlange (f) *music*
   system; **Musikinstrument** (nt)
   musical instrument
Musiker(in) *musician*
mussen *to have to* (must);
   ich muss... *I must...*
Mutter (f) *mother; nut* (for bolt)
Mütze (f) *cap* (hat)

N

nach *after, towards;* **nach**
   England *to England*
Nachname (m) *surname*
Nachricht (f) *message*
Nachrichten *news*

nächster *next;*
   nächste Woche *next week*
Nacht (f) *night*
Nachthemd (nt) *nightdress*
Nachtisch (m) *desserts*
Nachtklub (m) *nightclub*
Nachtportier (m) *night porter*
Nachttisch (m) *bedside table*
Nadel (f) *needle*
Nagel (m) *nail* (metal, finger);
   Nagelfeile (f) *nailfile;*
   Nagellack (m) *nail polish;*
   Nagelzwicker (m)
   nail clippers
nah *close, near;* **nahe der Tür**
   near the door; **in der**
   Nähe von London
   near London
nähen *to sew*
Name (m) *name*
Nase (f) *nose*
naß *wet*
Nebel (m) *fog*
neben *beside*
Neffe (m) *nephew*
Negativ (nt) *negative* (photo)
nehmen *take*
nein *no* (response)
neu *new*
neun *nine*
neunzehn *nineteen*
neunzig *ninety*
Neuseeland *New Zealand*
Neuseeländer(in) (m/f)
   New Zealander
nicht *not;*
   nicht so viel *not so much;*
   nicht viele *not many*
Nichte (f) *niece*
nichts *nothing*
nie *never*
Niederlande: die Niederlande
   the Netherlands
niedrig *low*
Niere (f) *kidney*
nirgendwo *nowhere*
noch ein *another one;*
   noch einen Kaffee,
   bitte *another coffee, please*
nochmal *again;*
   nochmal dasselbe, bitte
   same again, please
noch nicht *not yet*
Nockenwelle (f) *camshaft*
Norden (m) *north*
Nordirland *Northern Ireland*
Nordsee: die Nordsee
   North Sea
Notausgang (m) *emergency exit*
Notbremse (f) *emergency brake*
Notfall (m) *emergency*

nötig: das ist nicht nötig
there's no need
Notizblock (m) *notepad*
Notizbuch (nt) *notebook*
notwendig *necessary*
November *November*
Nudeln (f) *pasta*
Nummer (f) *number;*
Nummernschild (nt)
number plate
nur *just, only*
Nuss (f) *nut (fruit)*

O

ob *whether*
oben *up;*
nach oben *upwards;*
da oben *up there*
Ober (m) *waiter;*
Herr Ober! *waiter!*
Obst (nt) *fruit*
oder *or*
offen *open (adj)*
öffentlich *public*
öffnen *to open*
Öffnungszeiten
opening times
oft *often*
ohne *without*
ohnmächtig werden
to faint
Ohr (nt) *ear;*
Ohren (nt pl) *ears*
Ohrringe (m pl) *earrings*
okay *OK*
Oktober *October*
Öl (nt) *oil*
Olive (f) *olive*
Omelette (nt) *omelette*
Onkel (m) *uncle*
Oper (f) *opera*
Operation (f) *operation*
Operationssaal (m)
operating theatre
Orange (f) *orange (fruit);*
orange *orange (colour)*
Orangenmarmelade (f)
marmalade
Orangensaft (m)
orange juice
Orchester (nt) *orchestra*
Ort (m) *place*
(town, etc.)
Osten (m) *east*
Österreich *Austria*
Österreicher(in) (m/f)
Austrian (person);
österreichisch
Austrian (adj)
Ostsee (f) *Baltic Sea*

P

Paar (nt) *pair*
Packpapier (nt) *wrapping paper*
Paket (nt) *package, packet, parcel*
Palast (m) *palace*
Panne (f) *breakdown (car)*
Pantoffeln (m pl) *slippers*
Papier (nt) *paper*
Paprika (m) *pepper*
(red/green)
Paraffin (nt) *paraffin*
Parfüm (nt) *perfume*
Park (m) *park*
parken *to park;* **Parken
verboten** *no parking*
Parkplatz (m) *car park*
Partei (f) *party (political,*
celebration)
Pass (m) *passport*
Passagier (m) *passenger*
passen Sie auf! *be careful!*
Passkontrolle (f)
passport control
Passwort (nt) *password*
peinlich *embarrassing*
Penizillin (nt) *penicillin*
perfekt *perfect*
Perle (f) *pearl*
Petersilie (f) *parsley*
Pfannkuchen (m) *pancake*
Pfeffer (m) *pepper (spice)*
Pfefferminzbonbons
(f) *peppermints*
Pfeife (f) *pipe (for smoking)*
Pfirsich (m) *peach*
Pflanze (f) *plant*
Pflaster (nt) *plaster (for cut)*
Pforte (f) *gate (garden gate)*
Pfund (nt) *pound*
(money, weight)
Picknick (nt) *picnic*
Pik *spades (cards)*
Pilot(in) (m/f) *pilot*
Pilz (m) *mushroom*
Pinsel (m) *paint brush*
Pinzette (f) *tweezers*
Pistole (f) *gun (pistol)*
Plastik (nt) *plastic*
Plastiktüte (f) *plastic bag*
Platten (m) *flat tyre*
Platz (m) *place, square*
(in town)
Plätzchen (nt) *biscuit*
Pole (m) *Pole (man)*
Polen *Poland*
Polin (f) *Pole (woman)*
Politik (f) *politics*
Polizei (f) *police*
Polizeibericht (m)
police report

Polizeirevier (nt)
police station
Polizist(in) (m/f)
police officer
polnisch *Polish*
Pommes (m pl) *chips*
Popmusik (f) *pop music*
Porrée (m) *leeks*
Portemonnaie (nt) *purse*
Portier (m) *porter (hotel)*
Portwein (m) *port (drink)*
Porzellan (nt) *china*
Post (f) *mail, post*
Postamt (nt) *post office*
Poster (nt) *poster*
Postkarte (f) *postcard*
Postleitzahl (f) *postcode*
Preis (m) *price*
prima! *great!*
privat *private*
pro *per;* **pro Nacht** *per night*
Problem (nt) *problem*
Professor(in) (m/f) *professor*
prost! *cheers!*
Prothese (f) *dentures,*
false teeth
Puder (m) *powder (cosmetics),*
talcum powder
Pullover (m) *jumper*
Pulver (nt) *powder*
Pulverkaffee (m) *instant coffee*
Pumpe (f) *pipe (for water)*
Puppe (f) *doll*
Putzfrau (f) *cleaner*

Q, R

Quadrat (nt) *square (shape)*
Qualität (f) *quality*
Qualle (f) *jellyfish*
Quittung (f) *receipt*
Rad (nt) *wheel*
radfahren *to cycle*
Radiergummi (m)
rubber (eraser)
Radieschen (nt) *radish*
Radio (nt) *radio*
Rang (m) *circle*
Rasen (m) *lawn*
Rasenmäher (m) *lawnmower*
Rasiercreme (f) *shaving foam*
rasieren: sich rasieren
to shave
Rasierklingen (f pl)
razor blades
Rasierwasser (nt) *aftershave*
Rathaus (nt) *town hall*
Ratte (f) *rat*
Rauch (m) *smoke*
rauchen *to smoke*
Raum (m) *room (space)*

Rechen (m) *rake*
Rechner (m) *calculator*
Rechnung (f) *bill, invoice*
recht (gut) *fairly (good)*
rechts *right (direction);* rechte
    Seite (f) *right side*
Rechtsanwalt/
    Rechtsanwältin (m/f) *lawyer*
reden *to talk*
Regen (m) *rain*
Regenmantel (m) *raincoat*
Regenschirm (m) *umbrella*
Regierung (f) *government*
reich *rich*
reif *ripe*
Reifen (m) *tyre*
Reifenpanne (f) *puncture*
Reinigung (f) *dry cleaner*
Reis (m) *rice*
Reise (f) *journey*
Reisebüro (nt) *travel agency*
Reiseführer (m) *guidebook*
Reiseleiter(in) (m/f)
    tour guide
Reißnagel (m) *drawing pin*
Reißverschluß (m) *zip*
Rekord (m) *record (sporting, etc.)*
Religion (f) *religion*
Reservierung (f) *reservation*
Rest (m) *rest (remainder)*
Restaurant (nt) *restaurant*
Rettich (m) *radish*
Rezept (nt) *prescription*
Rhabarber (m) *rhubarb*
richtig *right (correct)*
riechen *to smell;*
    Das riecht gut
    that smells good
Riegel (m) *bolt (on door)*
Rindfleisch (nt) *beef*
Ring (m) *ring (jewellery)*
Rock (m) *skirt; rock (music)*
Rohr (nt) *pipe (for water)*
Rollstuhl (m) *wheelchair*
Rollstuhlfahrer (m)
    wheelchair access
Rolltreppe (f) *escalator*
Roman (m) *novel*
Röntgenabteilung (f)
    x-ray department
Röntgenaufnahme (f) *x-ray*
rosa *pink*
Rose (f) *rose*
Rosinen (f pl) *raisins*
rot *red*
Rubin (m) *ruby (gem)*
Rücken (m) *back (body)*
Rückfahrkarte (f)
    return ticket
Rücklichter (f pl) *rear lights*
Rucksack (m) *rucksack*

Rückseite (f) *back (not front)*
rufen *to shout*
ruhig *quiet*
Ruinen (f pl) *ruins*
Rum (m) *rum*
rund *round (circular)*
Rundreise (f) *tour*

S

sagen *to say;*
    was haben Sie gesagt?
    what did you say?;
    wie sagt man...?
    how do you say...?
Sahne (f) *cream*
    (for cake, etc.)
Saite (f) *string (guitar, etc.)*
Salami (f) *salami*
Salat (m) *salad*
Salbe (f) *ointment*
Salz (nt) *salt*
Sammlung (f) *collection*
    (stamps, etc.)
Samstag *Saturday*
Sand (m) *sand*
Sandalen (f pl) *sandals*
Sandwich (nt) *sandwich*
Satellitenfernsehen (nt)
    satellite TV
satt: ich bin satt *I'm full (up)*
sauber *clean*
Sauna (f) *sauna*
Schach *chess*
Schachtel (f) *box, packet;*
    Schachtel Pralinen (f)
    box of chocolates
Schaffner (m) *conductor (bus)*
Schal (m) *scarf*
Schallplatte (f) *record (music)*
Schallplattengeschäft (nt)
    record shop
Schalter (m) *switch; ticket kiosk*
Schaltknüppel (m) *gear lever*
Schauer (m) *shower (rain)*
Schaumfestiger (m) *mousse*
    (for hair)
Scheck (m) *cheque*
Scheckheft (nt) *chequebook*
Scheckkarte (f) *cheque card*
Scheinwerfer (m pl) *headlights*
Scheitel (m) *parting (hair)*
Schere (f) *scissors*
Schiff (nt) *boat, ship*
Schild (nt) *sign*
Schlaf (m) *sleep*
Schlafanzug (m) *pyjamas*
schlafen *to sleep*
Schlaflosigkeit (f) *insomnia*
Schlafsack (m) *sleeping bag*
Schlaftablette (f) *sleeping pill*

Schlafzimmer (nt) *bedroom*
Schlange (f) *queue*
Schlauch (m) *inner tube*
schlecht *bad, poor (quality)*
schlechter *worse*
schlechtester *worst*
schleudern *to skid*
schließen *to close*
Schlitten (m) *sledge, toboggan*
Schlittschuhe *ice skates;*
    Schlittschuh laufen gehen
    to go ice-skating
Schloss (nt) *castle*
Schlüssel (m) *key*
Schlussverkauf (m) *sale*
    (at reduced prices)
Schmerz (m) *ache, pain*
Schmerztablette (f) *painkiller*
Schmuck (m) *jewellery*
schmutzig *dirty*
Schnee (m) *snow*
schneiden *to cut*
schnell *fast, quick*
Schnellimbiss (m) *take-away*
Schnitt (m) *cut*
Schnuller (m) *dummy*
    (for baby)
Schnurrbart (m) *moustache*
Schnürsenkel (m pl) *shoelaces*
Schokolade (f) *chocolate*
schon *already, yet;*
    ist es schon fertig?
    is it ready yet?
schön *beautiful, pretty*
Schornstein (m) *chimney*
Schotte (m) *Scotsman*
Schottin (f) *Scotswoman*
schottisch *Scottish*
Schottland *Scotland*
Schrank (m) *cupboard*
Schraube (f) *screw*
Schraubenschlüssel (m)
    spanner
Schraubenzieher (m)
    screwdriver
schrecklich *horrible*
Schreibmaschine (f) *typewriter*
Schreibpapier (nt)
    writing paper
Schreiner(in) *carpenter*
Schublade (f) *drawer*
Schuhcreme (f) *shoe polish*
Schuhe (m pl) *shoes*
Schuhgeschäft (nt) *shoe shop*
Schule (f) *school*
Schulter (f) *shoulder*
Schüssel (f) *bowl*
schwager *pregnant*
Schwager (m) *brother-in-law*
Schwägerin (f) *sister-in-law*
schwarz *black*

schwarze Johannisbeere (f) *blackcurrant*

Schwarzwald (m) *Black Forest*

Schweinefleisch (nt) *pork*

Schweiß (m) *sweat*

Schweiz: die Schweiz *Switzerland*

Schweizer(in) (m/f) *Swiss (person)*

schweizerisch *Swiss* (adj)

schwer *heavy, hard* (difficult)

Schwester (f) *sister*

schwierig *difficult*

Schwimmbad (nt) *swimming pool*

Schwimmen (nt) *swimming;* **schwimmen** *to swim*

Schwimmflossen (f pl) *flippers*

schwitzen *to sweat*

schwul *gay* (homosexual)

sechs *six*

sechzehn *sixteen*

sechzig *sixty*

See (m) *lake*

Segelboot (nt) *sailing boat*

Segeln (nt) *sailing*

sehen *to see;* **ich kann nichts sehen** *I can't see*

sehr *very*

Seide (f) *silk*

Seife (f) *soap*

Seil (nt) *rope*

sein(e) *his*

Seite (f) *page, side*

Sekratär(in) (m/f) *secretary*

Sekunde (f) *second* (time)

selbständig *self-employed*

selten *rare* (uncommon)

Seminar (nt) *seminar*

Senf (m) *mustard*

September *September*

Serviette (f) *napkin, serviette*

Sessel (m) *armchair*

setzen *put*

Shampoo (nt) *shampoo*

Sherry (m) *sherry*

Shorts (f) *shorts*

sicher *safe, sure;* **Sicherheitsgurt** (m) *seat belt;* **Sicherheitsnadel** (f) *safety pin*

Sie *you* (singular, formal); **sie** *she/they*

sieben *seven*

siebzehn *seventeen*

siebzig *seventy*

Silber (nt) *silver* (metal); **silber** *silver* (colour)

sind: wir/sie/Sie sind; *we/they/you* (formal) *are*

Singen (nt) *singing;* **singen** *to sing*

Sirup (m) *syrup*

Sitz (m) *seat*

Skandinavien *Scandinavia*

Skibindung (f) *ski binding*

Skier (m pl) *skis*

Ski fahren *to ski;* **Skifahren gehen** *to go skiing*

Skilift (m) *ski lift*

Skistiefel (m pl) *ski boots*

Skistöcke (m pl) *ski sticks*

Skiurlaubsort (m) *ski resort*

Smaragd (m) *emerald*

so *like this, so*

Socken (f pl) *socks*

Sodawasser (nt) *soda water*

Sofa (nt) *sofa*

sofort *immediately*

Sohn (m) *son*

Sonderangebot (nt) *bargain*

Sonne (f) *sun*

sonnenbaden *to sunbathe*

Sonnenbrand (m) *sunburn*

Sonnenbrille *sunglasses*

Sonnenöl (nt) *suntan lotion*

Sonnenschirm (m) *sunshade*

sonnig *sunny*

Sonntag *Sunday*

sorgfältig *careful*

Soße (f) *sauce*

Souvenir (nt) *souvenir*

sowohl... als auch... *both... and...*

spät *late*

Spaten (m) *spade* (shovel)

später *later*

spazieren gehen *to go for a walk*

Spaziergang (m) *walk* (stroll)

Speck (m) *bacon*

Speisekarte (f) *menu*

Speiseraum (m) *dining room*

Spiegel (m) *mirror*

Spiel (nt) *match* (sport)

spielen *to play*

Spielzeug (nt) *toy*

Spinat (m) *spinach*

Spinne (f) *spider*

Spitze (f) *lace; tip* (end)

Sport (m) *sport;* **Sportzentrum** (nt) *sports centre*

Sportwagen (m) *pushchair*

Sprache (f) *language*

Sprachführer (m) *phrase book*

sprechen *to speak;* **sprechen Sie Englisch?** *do you speak English?;* **ich spreche kein Deutsch** *I don't speak German*

Spritze (f) *injection, syringe*

sprudelnd *fizzy*

Sprung (m) *dive*

Sprungbett (nt) *diving board*

Spülmittel (nt) *washing-up liquid*

stabil *strong, stable* (material)

Stadion (nt) *stadium*

Stadt (f) *town, city*

Stadtplan (m) *town plan, map*

Stadtrand (m) *suburbs*

Stadtzentrum (nt) *city/city centre*

Stand (m) *stand*

Standlicht (nt) *sidelights*

Star (m) *star* (film)

stark *strong* (person, drink)

Start (m) *start*

Start-und Landebahn (f) *runway*

Station *station* (underground)

Statue (f) *statue*

Stau (m) *traffic jam*

Staubsauger (m) *vacuum cleaner*

Staubtuch (nt) *duster*

Steak (nt) *steak*

stechen *to bite, sting* (insect)

Stecker (m) *plug* (electrical)

Stecknadel (f) *pin*

stehlen *to steal;* **es ist gestohlen worden** *it's been stolen*

steht: es steht Ihnen *it suits you*

Stein (m) *rock* (stone)

stellen *to put*

Steppdecke (f) *duvet*

sterben *to die*

Stern (m) *star*

Stich (m) *bite, sting* (by insect)

stickig *close* (stuffy)

Stiefel (m) *boot* (footwear)

Stiefmutter (f) *stepmother*

Stiefsohn (m) *stepson*

Stieftochter (f) *stepdaughter*

Stiefvater (m) *stepfather*

Stift (m) *pen*

still *quiet*

stillhalten! *don't move!*

Stimme (f) *voice*

Stock (m) *floor* (storey)

Stoff (m) *material* (fabric)

Stöpsel (m) *plug* (sink)

Stoßstange (f) *bumper*

Strand (m) *beach*

Straße (f) *road, street*

Straßenbahn (f) *tram*

Streichholz (nt) *match* (light)

streng *strong* (taste)

stricken *to knit*

Strickwaren (f pl) *knitwear*

Strom (m) *electricity*

Stromanschluss (m) *electrical hook-up*

Strümpfe (m pl) stockings
Strumpfhose (f) tights
Stück (nt) piece, slice, play (theatre); **fünf Euro das Stück** five euros each
Student(in) (m/f) student
Stuhl (m) chair
Stunde (f) hour, lesson
Sturm (m) storm
Sucher (m) viewfinder
Südafrika South Africa
Süden (m) south
Supermarkt (m) supermarket
Suppe (f) soup
süß sweet (not sour)
Süßigkeit (f) sweet (candy)
Sweatshirt (nt) sweatshirt
Synagoge (f) synagogue

T

Tabak (m) tobacco
Tablett (nt) tray
Tablette (f) pill, tablet
Tafel Schokolade (f) bar of chocolate
Tafelwasser (nt) still water
Tag (m) day
Tagebuch (nt) diary
Tagesdecke (f) bedspread
Tagesordnung (f) agenda
Tal (nt) valley
Tampons (m pl) tampons
Tankstelle (f) petrol station
Tante (f) aunt
Tanz (m) dance
tanzen to dance
Tasche (f) pocket, bag
Taschendieb (m) pickpocket
Taschenlampe (f) torch
Taschenmesser (nt) penknife
Taschentücher tissues
Tasse (f) cup
Tastatur (f) keyboard
taub deaf
tauchen to dive
tauschen, umtauschen to exchange
tausend thousand
Taxi (nt) taxi
Taxistand (m) taxi rank
Technik (f) engineering
Tee (m) tea; **schwarze Tee** black tea; **Tee mit Milch** tea with milk
Teilchen (nt) danish pastry
Telefon (nt) telephone
Telefonbuch (nt) directory
telefonieren to telephone
Telefonkarte (f) phonecard
Telefonzelle (f) telephone box

Teller (m) plate
Temperatur (f) temperature
Tennis (nt) tennis
Teppich (m) carpet
Termin (m) appointment
Terminal (nt) terminal
Terrasse (f) terrace
Tesafilm (m) sellotape
teuer expensive, dear
Theater (nt) theatre
tief deep, low (voice)
Tiefkühlkost (f) frozen foods
Tierarzt (m) vet
Tierpass (m) pet passport
Tinte (f) ink
Tisch (m) table
Toast (m) toast
Tochter (f) daughter
Toilette (f) toilet
Toilettenpapier (nt) toilet paper
Tomate (f) tomato
Tomatensaft (m) tomato juice
Tonic (nt) tonic
Töpferei (f) pottery
Tor (nt) gate
tot dead
Tourist(in) (f) tourist
Tradition (f) tradition
Tragetasche (f) plastic bag
Trainingsanzug (m) track suit
Traktor (m) tractor
trampen to hitchhike
Trauben (f pl) grapes
traurig sad
Treffen (nt) meeting
Treppe (f) stairs, staircase
trinken to drink
Trinkgeld (nt) tip (money)
Trinkwasser (nt) drinking water
trocken dry
Tropfen (f) drops
Truhe (f) chest (furniture)
tun to do
Tunnel (m) tunnel
Tür (f) door
Türke Turk (man)
Türkin Turk (woman)
Türkei: die Türkei Turkey
türkisch Turkish
Turm (m) tower
Turnschuhe trainers

U

U-Bahn (f) underground, metro
U-Bahnstation (f) metro station
übel: mir ist übel I feel sick
über over, across, more than
überall everywhere

Überführung (f) flyover
überfüllt crowded
übergeben: sich übergeben to be sick (vomit)
überholen to overtake
Überlandbus (m) coach
übersetzen to translate
Übersetzer(in) (m/f) translator
Überzelt (nt) fly sheet
Uhr (f) clock, watch
um 3 Uhr at 3 o'clock
Umhängetuch (nt) shawl
umziehen to move (house)
umziehen: sich umziehen to change (clothes)
und and
Unfall (m) accident
Unfallstation (f) emergency department
ungewöhnlich unusual
Universität (f) university
Unkraut (nt) weeds
unmöglich impossible
unten down; **hier unten** down here
unter... below..., under...
Untergeschoss (nt) basement
Unterhaltung (f) entertainment
Unterhemd (nt) vest
Unterhose (f) underpants
Unterkunft (f) accommodation
Unterrock (m) underskirt
Untertasse (f) saucer
Unterwäsche (f) underwear
Urlaub (m) holiday

V

Vanille (f) vanilla
Vase (f) vase
Vater (m) father
Vegetarier(in) (m/f) vegetarian (person)
vegetarisch vegetarian (adj)
Ventil (nt) valve
Ventilator (m) fan (ventilator)
Verband (m) bandage
Verbrennung (f) burn
Vergaser (m) carburettor
vergessen to forget
Vergrößerung (f) enlargement
verheiratet married
Verhütungsmittel (nt) contraceptive
verkaufen to sell
Verkäufer(in) (m/f) shopkeeper
Verkehr (m) traffic
Verkehrsbüro (nt) tourist office
Verlängerungsschnur (f) extension lead

Verletzung (f) *injury*
verlobt *engaged (couple)*
Verlobte (m/f) *fiancé(e)*
Vermittlung (f) *operator*
verriegeln *to bolt*
verrückt *mad*
verschieden *different*
Verschluss (m) *cap (bottle), shutter (camera)*
Versicherung (f) *insurance*
verspätet *delayed*
Verspätung: der Bus hat Verspätung *the bus is late*
verstehen *understand;* **ich verstehe** *I see/I understand;* **ich verstehe nicht** *I don't understand*
versuchen *to try*
Vertrag (m) *contract*
Vertreter (m) *agent*
Verwandte (m) *relative*
Verzeihung! *sorry! (apology)*
Vetter (m) *cousin (male)*
Video (nt) *video*
Videocassette (f) *video tape*
Videorecorder (m) *video recorder*
viel *a lot, much*
vielleicht *maybe, perhaps*
vier *four*
Viertel (nt) *quarter*
vierter *fourth*
vierzehn *fourteen*
vierzig *forty*
Villa (f) *villa*
Visitenkarte (f) *business card*
Vitamintablette (f) *vitamin tablet*
Vogel (m) *bird*
Voice-mail (f) *voicemail*
Volksmusik (f) *folk music*
voll *busy (bar, etc.), full*
Vollpension *full board*
von *of*
vor... *before..., in front of...*
vorbei *over (finished)*
Vorgesetzte (m/f) *superior*
Vorhang (m) *curtain*
Vorhängeschloss (nt) *padlock*
Vorlesungssaal (m) *lecture theatre*
Vorname (m) *first name*
Vorspeisen (f pl) *starters*
Vortrag (m) *presentation*

W

Wächter (m) *guard*
Wagen (m) *carriage (train)*
wahr *true*
während *during*
Wald (m) *forest*
Wales *Wales*
Waliser(in) (m) *Welshman/ Welshwoman*
walisisch *Welsh*
Wand (f) *wall (inside)*
Wandern (nt) *hiking*
Wandteppich (m) *tapestry*
wann? *when?*
war *was;* **ich war** *I was;* **er/sie/es war** *he/she/it was*
waren *were;* **wir/sie waren** *we/they were;* **Sie waren** *you (formal) were*
warm *warm*
warst *were;* **du warst** *you (informal) were*
warten *wait;* **warten Sie!** *wait!*
Wartesaal (m) *waiting room (station)*
Wartezimmer (nt) *waiting room*
warum? *why?*
was? *what?;* **was ist das?** *what's that/this?*
Waschbecken (nt) *wash basin*
Wäsche (f) *laundry (dirty clothes)*
Wäscheklammer (f) *clothes peg*
Wäscherei (f) *laundry (place)*
Waschpulver (nt) *washing powder*
Waschsalon (m) *launderette*
Wasser (nt) *water;* **Wasser mit Kohlensäure, das Sprudelwasser** *fizzy water;* **Wasser ohne Kohlensäure** *still water*
Wasserfall (m) *waterfall*
Wasserkessel (m) *kettle*
Watte (f) *cotton wool*
Webseite (f) *website*
Wechselkurs (m) *exchange rate*
wechseln *to change (money)*
Wecker (m) *alarm clock*
weder... noch... *neither... nor...*
Weg (m) *path*
weich *soft*
Weihnachten (nt) *Christmas*
weil *because*
Wein (m) *wine;* **Weinkarte** (f) *wine list*
Weinbrand (m) *brandy*

weinen *to cry (weep)*
weiß *white*
weit *far;* **wie weit ist es?** *how far is it?;* **ist es weit von hier?** *is it far away?*
welcher? *which?*
Welle (f) *wave*
wellig *wavy (hair)*
weniger *less*
wenn *if*
wer? *who?*
Werkstatt (f) *car repairs, garage*
Wertsachen (f pl) *valuables*
Wespe (f) *wasp*
Westen (m) *west*
Wetter (nt) *weather*
Whisky (m) *whisky*
wie? *how?;* **wie heißen Sie?** *what's your name?;* **wie spät ist es?** *what's the time?*
Wien *Vienna*
willkommen *welcome*
Wimperntusche (f) *mascara*
Wind (m) *wind*
Windel (f) *nappy*
Windschutzscheibe (f) *windscreen*
winken *to wave*
wir *we*
wissen *to know (a fact);* **ich weiß nicht** *I don't know*
Witz (m) *joke*
wo? *where?*
Woche (f) *week*
Wodka (m) *vodka*
Wohnmobil (nt) *camper van*
Wohnung (f) *apartment, flat*
Wohnwagen (m) *caravan*
Wohnzimmer (nt) *lounge (in house)*
Wolldecke (f) *rug (blanket)*
Wolle (f) *wool*
Wort (nt) *word*
Wörterbuch (nt) *dictionary*
Wurst (f) *sausage*

Z

Zahl (f) *number*
Zahn (m) *tooth*
Zahnarzt (m) *dentist*
Zahnbürste (f) *toothbrush*
Zahnpasta (f) *toothpaste*
Zahnschmerzen (f) *toothache*
Zäpfchen (nt) *suppository*
Zaun (m) *fence*
zehn *ten*
zehntausend *ten thousand*
Zeit (f) *time*
Zeitplan (m) *schedule*
Zeitschrift (f) *magazine*

Zeitung (f) *newspaper*
Zeitungsladen (m)
  newsagent's (shop)
Zelt (nt) *tent*
Zeltboden (m) *groundsheet*
Zeltstange (f) *tent pole*
Zentrale (f) *head office*
Zentralheizung (f)
  central heating
zerbrochen *broken* (vase, etc.)
Zeuge(in) (m/f) *witness*
ziehen *pull*
ziemlich *fairly, quite*
Zigarette (f) *cigarette*
Zigarre (f) *cigar*
Zimmer (nt) *room*
Zimmermädchen (nt) *maid*
Zimmerservice (m)
  room service
Zitrone (f) *lemon*
Zoll (m) *Customs*
zollfrei *duty-free*
Zoo (m) *zoo*
zu *too* (excessively)
Zucker (m) *sugar*
Zug (m) *train*
zum *to;* **zum Bahnhof**
  to the station
Zündkerze (f) *spark plug*
Zündung (f) *ignition*
Zunge (f) *tongue*
zurückgeben *to return*
  (give back)
zurückkommen *to return*
  (come back)
zusammen *together*
Zusammenbruch (m)
  nervous breakdown
Zuschlag (m) *supplement*
zwanzig *twenty*
Zweck (m) *purpose;* **es hat**
  keinen Zweck *it's no use*
zwei *two;*
  zwei Einzelbetten *twin beds;*
  zwei Wochen *fortnight*
Zweigstelle (f) *branch*
zweiter *second* (in series);
  zweiter Klasse *second class*
Zwiebel (f) *onion*
zwischen... *between...*
zwölf *twelve*

Acknowledgments

The publisher would like to thank the following for their help in the preparation of this book: Edith and Dieter Gollnow for the organization of location photography in Germany; Die Bahn DB, Deutsche Bahn AG, Hannover; Üstra Hannoversche Verkehrsbetriebe AG, Hannover; Raustaurant: Der Gartensaal im Neuen Rathaus, Hannover; Sprengel-Museum Hannover; Polizei-Direktion Hannover; Café An der Martkirche, Hannover; Teestübchen Am Ballhof; Europa-Apotheke, Hannover; Wochenmarkt Gretchenstraße; Magnet Showroom, Enfield; MyHotel, London; Kathy Gammon; Juliette Meeus and Harry.

Language content for Dorling Kindersley by **g-and-w publishing**
Managed by **Jane Wightwick**
Editing and additional input: **Sam Fletcher, Christopher Wightwick**

Additional design assistance: **Lee Riches, Fehmi Cömert, Sally Geeve**
Additional editorial assistance: **Paul Docherty, Mary Lindsay, Lynn Bresler**
Picture research: **Louise Thomas**

Picture credits

p2 Alamy: Chris Warham tr; p4/5 Alamy: Goodshoot tr; p6/7 Laura Knox: cl; p10/11 Alamy: BananaStock cAr, bl; RubberBall cBl; p12/13 Alamy: John Foxx cAr; RubberBall br; DK Images: cl; Steve Shott cBr; Ingram Image Library: tr, cr; p14/15 Alamy: Comstock Images tcr; Dreamstime.com: Slobodan Mračina (cl); Ingram Image Library: cl; p16/17 Alamy: RubberBall bcr; Ingram Image Library: tr; p18/19 Alamy: Foodfolio cr; DK Images: David Murray tr; Ian O'Leary clB; p22/23 Alamy: Image Source crA; Think Stock bcl; DK Images: cl, Susanna Price br; Magnus Rew tcrB; Ingram Image Library: tcr; p24/25 Alamy: Archivberlin Fotoagentur GmbH clA, Dave King tcr; p26/27 Ingram Image Library: cl; p28/29 DK Images: Dave King cr; Stephen Oliver tr; Matthew Ward bclA; Ingram Image Library: bcrA, bcr; p30/31 Alamy: Comstock Images bcl; DK Images: cl, bclA; Andy Crawford crA; p34/35 Dreamstime.com: Slobodan Mračina (cb); Ingram Image Library: tcr; iStockphoto.com: nicolas_ (tl); p36/37 DK Images: bcl, bcr; Magnus Rew cl; Dreamstime.com: Slobodan Mračina (cla); Ingram Image Library: bl; iStockphoto.com: nicolas_ (cla/sim card); p38/39 Alamy: Imageshop / Zefa Visual Media cl; p40/41 Alamy: Archiv Fotoagentur GmbH bcr; DK Images: Dorota and Mariusz Jarymowicz cl; p42/43 Alamy: Michael Klinec tcrB; Alamy: Comstock Images cAr; Goodshoot tcr; Nigel Schermuly: cr; p44/45 Courtesy of Audi UK c; p46/47 Alamy: Imageshop / Zefa Visual Media br; Courtesy of Audi UK: tcr; DK Images: Dorota and Mariusz Jarymowicz bcl, bcr; Ingram Image Library: tclB; Nigel Schermuly: cr; p48/49 Alamy: Chris Warham c; DK Images: Dorota and Mariusz Jarymowicz c; p50/51 Alamy: Andre Jenny c; p52/53 Alamy: Pat Behnke tcrB; Alamy: Image Farm Inc cAr; DK Images: Steve Gorton tcrB; p54/55 Alamy: Jackson Smith bclA; Alamy: BananaStock cl; John Foxx c; Image Source cAr; ThinkStock tcr; DK Images: Andy Crawford cr; p56/57 Alamy: Goodshoot clA; Chris Warham cl; Courtesy of Audi UK: bc; DK Images: Dorota and Mariusz Jarymowicz tl, clAA; p58/59 Alamy: Michael Juno tcr; Alamy: Brand X Pictures cBl, cBBl; Image Source cAAl; DK Images: cAl; p60/61 123RF.com: shutswis (cb); Alamy: Robert Harding Picture Library bcr; Alamy: imagebroker bl; Image Source cAr; DK Images: Steve Gorton tcrB; Pia Tryde cAAr; Ingram Image Library: cr; p62/63 DK Images: Stephen Whitehorn c; p64/65 Alamy: Arcaid bcrA; Dennis Hallinan c; Alamy: GKPhotography cBr; Goodshoot cAAr; Justin Kase tcrB; DK Images: Steve Tanner cAr; Ingram Image Library: tcr; p66/67 Alamy: Arcaid tl; Alamy: Image Source cAr; DK Images: tr; Stephen Whitehorn bl; Ingram Image Library: br; p68/69 Alamy: Balearic Pictures cr; Alamy: Celestial Panoramas cAl; p70/71 Ingram Image Library: cr; p72/73 Alamy: imagebroker tcrB; Image Source cAr; Comstock Images tcr; Elizabeth Whiting & Associates bl; p74/75 Alamy RF: Doug Norman bl; Ingram Image Library: c; p76/77 Alamy: Balearic Pictures cBl; Alamy: Celestial Panoramas Ltd bcl; p80/81 Getty: Taxi / Rob Melnychuk bc; Ingram Image Library: cAr; Xerox UK Ltd: tcr; p82/83 Alamy: wildphotos.com tcr; Alamy: FogStock cAAl; Momentum Creative Group cAl; Shoosh / Up the Res cBl; Ingram Image Library: cl; p84/85 Alamy: Brand X Pictures cr; f1 Online c; Alamy RF: image100 bl; SuperStock tr; Ingram Image Library: crB; p86/87 Getty: Taxi / Rob Melnychuk tc; p90/91 Alamy: Brand X Pictures tcr; DK Images: cl; David Jordan cAr; Stephen Oliver cr; Ingram Image Library: cBr; p92/93 Alamy: Pixland cr; DK Images: cl; Guy Ryecart tr; p94/95 Alamy: David Kamm cl; Phototake Inc bcl; Alamy: Comstock Images cr; ImageState Royalty Free bcr; DK Images: Stephen Oliver tcr; p96/97 Alamy: Pixland br; DK Images: tl; Ingram Image Library: tr; p98/99 Alamy: Bildarchiv Monheim GmbH / Jochen Helle c; Alamy: ThinkStock br; DK Images: Jake Fitzjones bl; Dreamstime.com: Alexandre Dvihally (tl); p100/101 DK Images: Steve Gorton tcr; p102/103 Alamy: The Garden Picture Library tcr; cAAr; Hortus b; D Hurst tcrB; Ingram Image Library: cAr; p104/105 DK Images: Paul Bricknell cl(6); Jane Burton bcl; Geoff Dann cl(2); Max Gibbs cl(4); Frank Greenaway cl(3); Dave King cl(1), cAr; Tracy Morgan c(5); p106/107 Alamy: The Garden Picture Library br; DK Images: Peter Kindersley cr; p108/109 Alamy: John Foxx tcr; p110/111 Alamy: RubberBall cr; DK Images: Andy Crawford cl; p112/113 Alamy RF: Image Source cl; DK Images: Dave King bcl; Steve Shott bl; Ingram Image Library: bcrA; p114/115 Alamy: FogStock tcr; Alamy: Image Source cAr; Index Stock cAl; p116/117 Alamy: The Garden Picture Library cAl; Alamy: clB; p118/119 DK Images: Steve Gorton tcr; GettyNews: Giuseppe Cacace c; p120/121 Alamy: ImageState / Pictor International cl; Shotfile cBl; Alamy: Sarkis Images tcr; DK Images: bcl; p122/123 Alamy: BananaStock cA; Ingram Image Library: cl; p124/125 Alamy: ImageState / Pictor International bclA; Shotfile cBl; DK Images: bcl; Paul Bricknell tc(5); Geoff Dann tc(3); Max Gibbs tc(1); Frank Greenaway tc(2); Dave King tc(4); Tracy Morgan tc(6); Ingram Image Library: bl; p126/127 Alamy: Pat Behnke blA; Alamy: Image Farm Inc cAr; p128 DK Images.

All other images **Mike Good.**